PENGUIN

Seafood

BIBLE

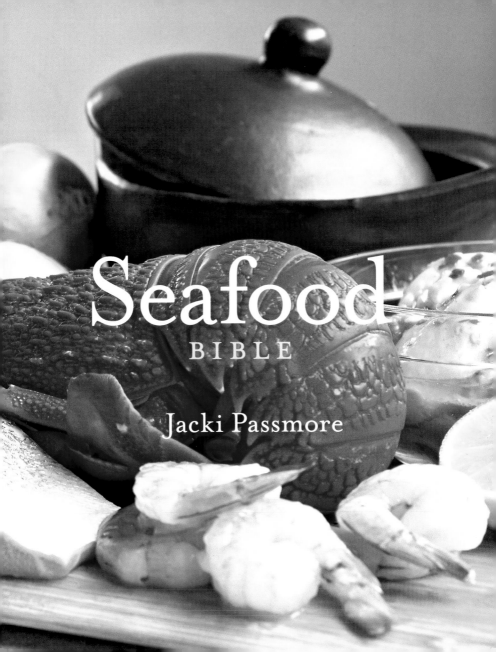

Seafood
BIBLE

Jacki Passmore

Contents

Introduction

Australia is blessed with a rich variety of seafood, and literally hundreds of marine and freshwater species are harvested. Familiar favourites such as flake (gummy shark) and prawns, richer and more distinctive varieties like yellow-fin tuna and the Queensland mud crab, and delicate, sweet-fleshed delights such as lobsters or coral trout, are a mere drop in the ocean when it comes to the choices available.

Seafood lends itself to the full complement of cooking methods: steaming, poaching, deep-frying, pan-frying, baking and grilling/barbecuing. Fish and shellfish also marry well with a huge range of flavourings: garlic, lemons and limes, and Asian and Mediterranean herbs and spices, to name but a few. *Seafood Bible* lets you in on all these secrets, and more: it's packed to the gills with recipes both traditional and thoroughly contemporary, as well as useful information and tips on selecting, storing and preparing the catch of the day.

Seafood basics

Seafood is a good source of protein and provides a swag of beneficial minerals and omega-3 fatty acids: nutritionists recommend that we consume one to four serves (100 g each) of seafood a week.

Seafood is not as tricky to cook as many people think. In fact, when it comes to a quick and fuss-free meal, you can't go past a grill, salad or stir-fry featuring your favourite fish.

Access to a reliable seafood supplier is a must: produce markets generally offer the best choice and the freshest ingredients, though most supermarkets stock a basic range. A good fishmonger will be a goldmine of information about what's freshest and/or at its seasonal best, and give you cooking advice as well. In these days of snap-freezing, frozen fish are not necessarily of poor quality, but the fact is that with seafood, fresh — very fresh — is definitely best.

What's on the menu?

These days, choosing fish for the table is not just about seeking out the freshest produce. We need to take account of the sustainability of our seas and of many of the species that are freely available at markets and fish suppliers. The issues are complex, from overfishing to methods of production (fish farmed in sea cages, for example) and harvesting. So do your homework before you go shopping, and avoid species that are of grave conservation concern. The Australian Marine Conservation Society has published a useful guide to choosing seafood wisely: www.amcs.org.au.

FINFISH

Finned fish come in all shapes and sizes, and vary also in terms of their oiliness, texture (dense, fine, soft, flaky), flavour (mild, medium, strong) and colour (white, pale pink, dark pink).

As a general rule, when grilling or barbecuing fish, opt for solid pieces such as steaks, cutlets or good-sized chunks. Soft-fleshed fish are best steamed. Thin or flat fish, and delicate fillets, are best pan-fried. Whole fish, especially large ones, are ideal for poaching or baking.

SHELLFISH

Shellfish, which include molluscs (clams, mussels, oysters, scallops) and crustaceans (bugs, crabs, crayfish/lobsters, prawns) and is sometimes extended to cephalopods (cuttlefish, octopus and squid), have long been a delicacy in many parts of the world.

Clams, mussels, oysters and scallops

There are several harvested *clam* species, perhaps the most common being the pipi, also known as the Coorong or Goolwa cockle, whose flesh is strongish in flavour and can at times be tough. Its relative the sand cockle (often known as *vongole*, the Italian word for clams) is a member of the venus-shell family. Its flesh is medium-flavoured, moist and relatively firm. Pipis and cockles can be substituted for each other, and for mussels, in many recipes.

The two main varieties of *mussel* available are the black-lip mussel (also called the blue mussel), with ebony-coloured shells and creamy, mild-tasting meat. The green-lip mussel, from New Zealand, is larger and slightly stronger in flavour. Some people prefer to remove the rubbery frill around the edge of the mussel meat.

There are three local *oyster* species, the most popular being the Sydney rock oyster (which is in fact grown along the coast from Victoria to Queensland). Its flesh is rich and creamy. The larger Pacific oyster, often called the Tasmanian oyster, has a firmish texture and a sweet, creamy flavour. The native flat oyster (or mud oyster) is believed by many cooks to have the tastiest flesh.

Cuttlefish, octopus and squid

There are about ten species of *cuttlefish* found in Australian waters. Cuttlefish have broader bodies than their relatives, squid and calamari, and the flesh has a firm texture and mild flavour. Cuttlefish ink is the traditional colourant for black pasta.

Octopus is harvested right around the Australian coast. It has a mild flavour and a denser texture than squid/calamari and cuttlefish. Marinating octopus before cooking helps to both flavour and tenderise it, though suppliers often sell octopus already tenderised. Baby octopus (usually with a body less than 10 cm long) are now commonly available and are a good option for the home cook; if you can't source them, use squid rings or pieces of octopus tentacle instead.

The terms *squid* and *calamari* are often used interchangeably, in part because calamari is the Italian word for 'squid', though experts generally define calamari as species with long, flap-like fins that extend the full length of the body. Squid and calamari, which are firm-textured and mild in flavour, can be cooked with the skin on (it turns dark purple as it cooks).

Bugs, crabs, lobsters and prawns
These crustaceans can be used interchangeably in most recipes.

There are two main *bug* species available commercially: the Balmain bug and the Moreton Bay bug. The edible flesh is found in the tail. In both species the flesh is firm and has a sweet, rich flavour (the Moreton Bay bug is slightly milder).

Although there are a number of native *crab* species, the three main food varieties are the blue swimmer crab, which has mild, sweet-tasting flesh; the mud crab, also sweet-fleshed but a little richer in flavour and firmer in texture; and the spanner crab, prized by many cooks for its succulent flesh.

Crayfish, which group includes yabbies and marrons, are freshwater relatives of the lobster. The spiny lobster (or *rock lobster*, as it is generally known in the southern hemisphere), which is abundant in Australasian waters, is only distantly related to the large-clawed family known in northern climes as the 'true' lobster. Rock lobsters are sold whole, live or cooked, and the tails are also available frozen.

About eight *prawn* species are harvested. They are sold either cooked or raw (green) and don't differ all that much in flavour. The most familiar are pink- or red-shelled king prawns, which vary markedly in size; banana prawns, readily available in northern regions, which are pale-coloured and have a light, sweet flavour; and the dramatically striped tiger prawns, which are among the largest species.

Buying and storing seafood

Seafood must be eaten fresh, preferably on the day you buy it. To keep it for more than a day, wrap in aluminium foil and store in the fridge for a maximum of three days.

Only buy frozen fish that you know was frozen soon after it was caught. The same goes for freezing seafood at home — it should be as fresh as possible. Frozen fish, or fish to be frozen, should be wrapped in plastic to avoid freezer burn, and should be kept for no more than three months. To thaw frozen fish, place it in a container lined with paper towels (or a draining rack), cover and leave in the refrigerator until thawed. Never thaw frozen fish at room temperature.

Whole fresh or frozen fish can be rinsed in running cold water, but it is best to not rinse fish fillets as they readily absorb water, which spoils their texture when cooked.

Finfish are most commonly sold whole or as fillets (lengthways, boneless slices). The skin becomes deliciously crisp and crunchy when grilled, so don't always opt for skinless fillets. Larger fish such as salmon are also sold as cutlets, a U-shaped piece cut crossways through the backbone and usually with the skin left on. They may also be sold as steaks about 10 mm thick.

SHELLFISH

Most crustaceans are sold already boiled and do not require further cooking. Frozen uncooked lobster, crab and prawn meat are also available. To store cuttlefish, squid and octopus, clean and then place in a plastic bag on a plate or tray or in a covered container in the refrigerator.

Where possible, buy live shellfish, for its superior flavour and texture. Oysters and mussels are commonly sold live, as are lobsters, yabbies and crabs in produce markets and specialist outlets. Bear in mind, though, that live lobsters and crabs, in particular, are hard to handle unless you are experienced (which is why their claws are tied for your safety). If you simply want to eat boiled lobster or crab, it is easier to buy them already cooked.

Live shellfish should be consumed as soon as possible after being caught or bought. To keep molluscs, mussels, lobsters and oysters alive, place in a container, cover with a damp teatowel, and leave in a cool part of the kitchen. In hot weather, prepare in the same way but keep in the warmest part of the refrigerator (usually the crisper drawer).

If buying ready opened oysters, choose specimens that look plump, moist and pale creamy-grey in colour. Experts argue that oysters should not be washed, that encountering the odd bit of grit or shell is preferable to rinsing away their special briny flavour.

Store unshelled raw or cooked prawns in a tub of crushed ice in the refrigerator for one to two days only; shelled prawns can be wrapped in plastic and covered with crushed ice. To freeze prawns in their shells, place in a plastic container and cover with clean water. Prawns should not be kept frozen for more than a few months.

KITCHEN TIPS

Many people are put off cooking fish because they don't care for its distinctive smell. If you belong to this club, here are a few solutions:

· Wear rubber or plastic gloves when shelling prawns.
· Clean your hands with stainless steel after preparing fish — buy a bar of stainless-steel soap, or simply rub your hands around the inside of a stainless-steel sink or bowl . . . Et voilà, the smells are gone! (Some people suggest that washing your hands with toothpaste, rather than soap, after handling seafood is another good way to get rid of the smell.)

- After purchasing seafood, store the discarded wrapping and parts (e.g. prawn shells) in the freezer until rubbish collection day.
- Run a citrus-based cleaning liquid down drains after preparing seafood.

You also need to think about hygiene safety when handling raw fish. To avoid cross-contamination with other foods, wash your hands before and after handling seafood, and keep utensils and work surfaces clean. In fact it's a good idea to wear disposable gloves when handling any seafood. And while you're preparing a dish, keep covered and chilled any seafood you're not working with.

Fish

In general, the more delicate fish respond best to simple cooking methods like pan-frying, and are great for puréeing (as with the fish terrines on page 36). Firm-textured species such as tuna respond well to braising, or can be sliced for stir-frying or sautéeing. Oily and/or stronger-flavoured fish love distinctive seasonings such as pepper, Asian or Middle Eastern spices, and take well to slow-cooking in the oven.

Salmon and ocean trout are interchangeable in all recipes, while tuna can replace firm-fleshed white fish (e.g. reef fish) in many dishes.

When buying tuna, look for soft dusky-pink flesh. Darker tuna has a stronger flavour, and is best for casseroles and baked dishes, although it also goes well with strong seasonings. (The dark-red section on some tuna cuts is called the blood line, and is usually trimmed away.)

Preparing and cooking fish

To be at their best, pink-fleshed fish such as salmon and tuna should be cooked succulently rare and barely warm in the centre, even when the outer surfaces are seared crisp and golden. To achieve this, cook until the flesh is visibly cooked to a depth of about 5–10 mm from the surface when viewed from the side (generally about 2 minutes) – then turn and cook the other side in the same way, leaving the centre a natural bright coral colour. You may, of course, cook these fish right through, but do not overcook as this will make them dry and unpalatable.

Fish with white or pale-pink flesh, such as rainbow trout, are best cooked right through. A good test for doneness is to pierce the thickest part of a fillet or whole fish with the blade of a knife. If the fish easily separates into flakes, or cuts through smoothly, it is cooked.

Baked fish with
preserved lemon & olives

2 medium-sized washed potatoes

3 tablespoons olive oil

4 tomatoes, sliced

salt and black pepper

600 g firm white fish fillets
(e.g. red snapper)

2 teaspoons ground cumin

2 teaspoons ground sweet
paprika

3 cloves garlic, crushed

3 tablespoons chopped fresh
parsley

3 tablespoons chopped fresh
coriander

3 slices preserved lemon peel,
chopped

⅓ cup chopped green olives

Pre-heat oven to 180°C.

Peel and thinly slice the potatoes, then boil in lightly salted water until
tender. Drain well.

Brush a large shallow casserole with olive oil and place the sliced potatoes
in the bottom, then layer half the tomatoes. Season lightly with salt and
pepper.

In a bowl combine a little salt and plenty of pepper, plus the cumin, paprika,
garlic, parsley and coriander. Season one side of each fish fillet with half
this mixture and place the fish (seasoned side down) over the tomatoes.
Scatter the remaining seasoning evenly over, and finish with the remaining
tomatoes. Evenly distribute the preserved lemon and the olives over the top

and drizzle with the remaining oil and plenty of pepper (but no more salt). Add ¾ cup water, cover with a lid or aluminium foil, and bake in preheated oven for 30 minutes.

After this time, uncover the casserole and bake another 15–20 minutes, until the fish feels tender when pierced with a knife.

Jars of preserved (salted) lemons are available at good delis and some supermarkets. To give this dish a crunchy topping, spread with fresh breadcrumbs when you uncover it after the first half hour in the oven. Dot with butter or olive oil, and return to the oven until the crust is golden-brown.

SERVES 6

Carpaccio of tuna
with capers & green olives

3 teaspoons shredded lemon zest

3 tablespoons extra-virgin olive oil

240 g boneless tuna

1 hard-boiled egg

1 small red onion, very finely chopped

10 jumbo green olives, pitted and diced

2 tablespoons baby capers, drained

basil leaves

black pepper

Place lemon zest in the olive oil and set aside to infuse.

Cut the tuna into paper-thin slices. (To make this easier, chill the tuna in the freezer until stiff, but not frozen.) Arrange tuna slices on four plates.

Peel the egg, separate the white from the yolk, and then chop (separately) finely.

Sprinkle the onion, olives, capers and chopped egg evenly over the tuna. Drizzle on the lemon-infused oil, then scatter with the basil leaves and pepper. Serve lightly chilled.

SERVES 4 AS AN ENTRÉE

Ceviche

200 g firm white fish fillets
(e.g. snapper or sea perch)

juice of 2 limes

1 fresh red chilli, deseeded
and chopped

2 tablespoons chopped fresh
coriander

1 teaspoon salt flakes

1 small carrot

1 small cucumber

½ small red onion, sliced

1 roma tomato, deseeded and
cut into thin strips

cos lettuce leaves, shredded

1 tablespoon avocado oil or
light olive oil

salt and pepper

With a very sharp knife, cut the fish into thin slices and spread in a shallow dish. Pour the lime juice over and scatter with the chilli, coriander and salt. Cover and refrigerate for 2–3 hours, turning once.

Peel the carrot and cucumber, and cut off thin strips of flesh with a vegetable peeler. Combine with the onion, tomato and lettuce. Toss the fish and its marinade with the salad and oil, and season with salt and pepper. Serve on chilled plates.

 Marinating fish in citrus juice effectively 'cooks' the flesh, making it tender, white and delicious.

SERVES 2–4

Clever little salmon soufflés

butter

white part of 1 spring onion, very finely chopped

220 g salmon fillets, skin removed

3 eggs, separated

2 teaspoons fish sauce

1 cup cream

salt and white pepper

Preheat oven to 200°C. Brush 6 small dishes (or 4 larger) with butter, brushing from the base to the top.

Place spring onion in a food processor with the salmon, 2 egg yolks, the fish sauce, cream and a little salt and pepper. Process to a creamy purée.

In a bowl whip the egg whites to stiff peaks. Stir a spoonful into the salmon cream, then carefully fold in the remainder.

Pile the mixture into the prepared dishes. Run a (clean) finger around the inside rim of each dish, which helps ensure that the soufflés rise evenly.

Place on a baking tray and bake in preheated oven for 15 minutes, until firm and puffed. **>**

Serve the soufflés hot in their dishes. Alternatively, run a knife around the inside of each dish and invert soufflés onto plates and surround with steamed spinach, asparagus or green beans tossed with lemon zest and butter.

You can refrigerate these soufflés for up to two days. To serve chilled, unmould and accompany with a tangy little salad garnished with orange or mandarin segments. Or serve them up the next day as 'twice-cooked soufflés': unmould and reheat in a hot oven (240°C) for 12 minutes.

SERVES 6 AS AN ENTRÉE (OR 4 AS A MAIN)

Crisp-fried fish in beer batter

1 cup plain flour

¾ teaspoon salt

3 tablespoons light olive oil

200 ml beer

600–700 g skinless fish fillets
 (e.g. snapper, john dory, flathead)

oil for deep-frying

1 egg white

tartare sauce (page 248) and lemon wedges, to serve

Sift the flour and salt into a bowl and make a well in the centre. Add the oil and gradually stir in the beer. Cover the batter and set aside for at least 1½ hours.

Pat fish dry with paper towels and cut each fillet lengthways in half. Pour oil into a pan suitable for deep-frying, and heat to 190°C.

Meanwhile, whisk the egg white to soft peaks and fold into the batter. It should be smooth and thin: if necessary, add a little more beer or water.

When the oil is ready, drag each strip of fish through the batter to coat well, and gently shake off any excess. Fry five or six pieces at a time, for about

4 minutes each, until golden and crisp. Drain on a rack over a dish covered with paper towels, and keep warm while you cook the rest.

Serve with tartare sauce and lemon wedges.

The egg white makes for a light and crisp batter. Aficionados like to use a full-flavoured beer, which adds depth of flavour without overwhelming the fish.

Crumbed fish fingers

500 g snapper or flathead fillets

1¼ cups plain flour

salt and pepper

4 cups oil for deep-frying

3 eggs, beaten

1½–2 cups fine dry breadcrumbs

tartare sauce (page 248), seafood sauce (page 247)
   or sweet chilli sauce

Dry the fish with paper towels and cut lengthways into strips as thick as a finger, then cut into 5-cm lengths.

Combine the flour, salt and pepper in a plastic or paper bag. Add the fish, hold bag closed and shake to coat the fish lightly. Tip fish into a colander and shake off any excess flour.

In a wok or large pan heat the oil to about 180°C. Dip the fish pieces into the egg, and then roll in breadcrumbs until lightly and evenly coated. (If time allows, refrigerate for 1 hour to set the crumbs before frying.)

Slide fish fingers carefully into the hot oil, about eight at a time, to fry for 1½–2 minutes or until the crumbs are golden. Lift out with a slotted spoon and drain on a rack over paper towels.   ❯

To serve as party finger food, serve the fish fingers on a tray lined with a napkin, and offer the sauces in little dishes for dipping. As an entrée, serve each person a few fish fingers, accompanied by a small herb and lettuce salad and a little pot of sauce for dipping. As a main course, serve the fish fingers over crisp-fried potato chips, with a sauce alongside.

 For fantastic fish burgers, fill a buttered long roll with shredded lettuce, a generous dollop of mayonnaise or tartare sauce, and three or four fish fingers.

MAKES ABOUT 24

Family fisherman's pie

350 g firm white fish fillets
(e.g. flake, ling)

salt and pepper

2 large potatoes

150 g mixed frozen peas
and corn

6 button mushrooms,
thinly sliced

½ onion, finely chopped

1 clove garlic, chopped

⅓ teaspoon crushed fennel
seeds

2 tablespoons butter

2 tablespoons plain flour

1 cup fish stock

3½ cup milk

2 tablespoons chopped
fresh parsley

Preheat the oven to 200°C.

Cut the fish into 2-cm cubes, season with salt and pepper, then set aside.

Peel and cube the potatoes, and boil in lightly salted water until tender.
Drain, mash with a little butter or milk, adding salt and pepper to taste,
then set aside. In another pan, parboil the peas and corn for 2 minutes
and then drain.

In a non-stick pan sauté the mushrooms, onion, garlic and fennel seeds in
2 tablespoons of the butter or oil for about 5 minutes over a medium-low
heat, until softened and lightly coloured. Add the flour and mix well, then
stir in the fish stock and the milk. Add the peas, corn, fish pieces and   >

parsley, then simmer, stirring carefully, until the sauce thickens
(2–3 minutes).

Spread the fish and vegetable mixture evenly in a pie dish and smooth
the top. Spoon mashed potato over, fluff up the surface with a fork and
dot with a few small cubes of butter. Bake for about 15 minutes, until
the fish is tender and the top golden-brown.

SERVES 4–6

Fish parcels

1 large clove garlic

½ teaspoon salt

2 anchovies, chopped

3 tablespoons butter

2 reef fish fillets (e.g. red
emperor) or barramundi

extra-virgin olive oil

black pepper

2 sprigs fresh rosemary

4 sprigs fresh thyme

2 sprigs fresh flat-leaf parsley

6 thin slices lemon

Preheat the oven to 190°C.

Mash the garlic with the salt, then mash with the anchovies and butter.

Prepare two large sheets of aluminium foil, cover each with a piece of
baking paper, then brush with olive oil. Fold in half, mark the centre and
then unfold. Place a piece of fish on each paper, butting against the fold.
Spread fish thickly with the garlic anchovy butter, then top with black
pepper, herb sprigs and lemon slices.

Make parcels, folding several times to ensure they are well sealed.
Don't make the parcels too tight, as they need space for trapped steam
to expand. Place parcels on an oven tray and place in preheated oven to
cook for 8-10 minutes: the parcels should puff out, owing to the steam
trapped inside. Slide onto plates to serve.

SERVES 2

Fish in wine butter sauce
with mushrooms

4 thick fillets of a firm fish such
  as mulloway, with skin on

2–3 tablespoons mild-flavoured
  oil

4 tablespoons butter

3 spring onions, white parts
  very finely chopped and
  green parts finely sliced

150 g button mushrooms,
  finely sliced

2–3 sprigs fresh thyme

2 teaspoons grated lemon zest

125 ml dry white wine
  or sparkling wine

salt and white pepper

3–4 teaspoons freshly
  squeezed lemon juice

2–3 tablespoons cream
  (optional)

Pat the fish dry with paper towels. Heat the oil in a non-stick pan and fry fish, skin side down, for about 4 minutes, then turn and fry on other side until cooked through (2–4 minutes). Transfer to a plate and keep warm.

Wipe out the pan and reheat, adding 1 tablespoon of the butter. Sauté the spring-onion whites and the mushrooms with the thyme for about 2 minutes. Add lemon zest, wine, and a large pinch each of salt and pepper. Simmer briskly for a few minutes to reduce, then whisk in the remaining butter a little at a time, until the sauce is glossy and slightly thickened. Add lemon juice, more salt and pepper to taste, and stir in the spring-onion greens. Add the cream, if using, just before serving.

SERVES 4

Fish terrines with lime hollandaise

3 white parts of spring onions, chopped

240 g skinless fillets of soft white fish (e.g. bream)

2 egg whites

2 tablespoons sour cream

2 teaspoons fish sauce

½ teaspoon salt

white pepper

squeeze of fresh lime juice

a little olive oil or melted butter

lime hollandaise (page 240)

lime wedges and sprigs of fresh dill, to serve

Place chopped spring-onion whites in a food processor. Cut the fish into cubes and add to the food processor with the egg whites, sour cream, fish sauce, salt and pepper, and lime juice. Purée to a very smooth and creamy paste, adding a little cold water if needed.

Brush small ramekins with the oil or butter and then line with cling wrap, allowing an overhang. Fill the pots with the fish mixture and fold the plastic wrap over, to cover.

Set a steamer over simmering water and put in the filled ramekins. Steam for about 10 minutes, or until the mixture is firm to the touch. Lift out the ramekins and set aside for a few minutes to allow the terrines to firm up further and cool to room temperature. >

To serve, turn out the terrines onto individual plates, cover with the hollandaise sauce and sprinkle with dill tips. Serve a lime wedge alongside.

The terrines can be made ahead and refrigerated for up to two days. For a change, serve with a garnish of chopped herbs and a little salad (e.g. orange segments with baby watercress leaves, tossed in a citrus vinaigrette).

SERVES 6

Garfish with Mediterranean herbs

12 garfish, cleaned and patted dry

⅓ cup plain flour, seasoned with salt and pepper

4 tablespoons olive oil

4 cloves garlic, peeled and slivered

4 sprigs fresh rosemary

4 sprigs fresh thyme

4 sprigs fresh oregano

⅓ cup red wine vinegar

extra salt (flakes) and freshly ground black pepper

Use a sharp knife to make several deep diagonal cuts on each side of the garfish. Coat lightly and evenly with the seasoned flour, brushing it into the cuts.

Heat the oil in a large frying pan and cook the fish, six at a time, until golden-brown (about 2½ minutes per side). Keep warm on a serving plate.

Drain oil from the pan (keep the oil), rinse the pan if needed, then return to the stove over a medium heat. Replace about 2 tablespoons of the oil in the pan and fry the garlic, rosemary, thyme and oregano for about   ➤

1½ minutes, until very fragrant. Deglaze the pan with the wine vinegar and pour over the fish. Season with salt and pepper, and serve.

 You could substitute small tailor fish or mullet for the garfish.

SERVES 4

Grilled bream with anchovy & lemon crumb crust

2 slices day-old ciabatta or sourdough bread,
  crusts removed

2–3 sprigs fresh parsley

2 strips lemon zest

1 clove garlic, peeled

2–4 anchovy fillets in oil, drained, chopped

salt and black pepper

1 tablespoon olive oil

2 skinless bream fillets (or reef fish such as red emperor)

Preheat grill to medium, or oven to hot (220°C).

Break bread into pieces and place in a food processor with the parsley, lemon zest and garlic. Grind to crumbs, then add the anchovy fillets, salt and pepper, and grind again briefly.

Heat oil in an ovenproof (metal-handled) frying pan and fry the fish fillets on one side for 1–2 minutes (depending on thickness). Spread seasoned breadcrumbs thickly over the fish and place under the grill or in the oven for about 5 minutes, until the crumbs are crisp and golden and the fish is cooked through. (Thicker fish pieces may need a little extra time.)

SERVES 2

Grilled sardines

24 small sardines, gutted
  (or use cleaned frozen
  sardines)
salt flakes

olive oil
freshly ground black pepper
  (optional)
lemon wedges, to serve

You can leave the heads on the sardines, or remove them, as preferred. Rinse well under running cold water, drain and pat dry. Sprinkle with salt, and set aside for 20 minutes.

Preheat a grill or barbecue to reasonably hot.

Brush the sardines with oil and cook for about 1 minute on one side (30–40 seconds for fillets), then turn and cook for another minute (30 seconds for fillets). Return whole fish briefly to the first side, season with salt and pepper, and serve at once with lemon wedges, fresh bread and a salad.

Anyone who has visited Spain, Portugal, Greece or anywhere around the Mediterranean will have enjoyed the simple pleasure of dining on grilled sardines straight from the fisherman's boat. For this dish, you need to source fresh sardines no longer than about 15 cm, and allow at least four per person. Frozen sardines are usually sold as double fillets.

SERVES 6

Japanese simmered mackerel

4 × 180-g mackerel steaks

⅔ cup sake (or ½ cup mirin)

2 tablespoons finely shredded
fresh ginger

a 7-cm piece daikon (or use
2–3 baby bok choy or
1 zucchini), thickly sliced

1 spring onion, sliced

salt

1½ tablespoons mirin (or use
sake plus 1 teaspoon sugar)

1½ tablespoons light soy sauce

⅔ cup dashi stock

Japanese shichimi (seven-spice)
seasoning

Rinse, drain and dry the fish.

Pour the sake into a pan (with a well-fitting lid) which will hold the fish in a
single layer. Scatter the ginger evenly into the pan with the sliced daikon,
bok choy or zucchini, and the spring onion. Arrange fish on top, sprinkle
lightly with salt, put lid on and cook for about 3 minutes.

After this time, pour the mirin, soy sauce and dashi stock into the pan and
simmer, uncovered, until the fish is tender (about 4 minutes).

Remove fish and vegetables to warm bowls and simmer the cooking liquid
for a further 4–5 minutes, until reduced a little. Pour sauce over the fish
and sprinkle generously with the shichimi seasoning. Serve with steamed
white rice.

SERVES 4

Lebanese whole baked salmon with sesame & herb dressing

1 whole salmon (at least 3 kg), scaled and cleaned

sea salt flakes and cracked black pepper

extra-virgin olive oil

DRESSING

½ cup tahini

1¼ cups creamy Greek-style yoghurt

½ cup extra-virgin olive oil

freshly squeezed juice of 1½–2 lemons, to taste

2–3 cloves garlic, mashed with a little salt

salt and cracked black pepper

GARNISH

¾ cup very finely chopped fresh flat-leaf parsley or coriander

¾ cup very finely chopped fresh dill, mint and/or basil

1 red onion, very finely chopped

grated zest of 2 lemons

1 fresh hot red chilli, deseeded and very finely chopped (optional)

Preheat oven to 150°C.

Season the fish, inside and outside, with salt and pepper.

Lay a large sheet of aluminium foil on a work surface and on top place a piece of baking paper a little larger than the fish. Set this in an oven tray, drizzle with oil, place the fish in the centre of the paper and drizzle with more oil. Pull up the edges of the foil to enclose the fish, folding the edges to seal.

Bake fish for 25 minutes in preheated oven, then turn parcel over carefully and bake for a further 25 minutes (fish larger than 3 kg will need an extra 5–10 minutes).

Take from the oven, open the foil, carefully remove the skin from the upper side of the fish and also gently scrape away the grey blood line.

Remove the fish head and discard. Place fish on a work surface: carefully separate the top fillet from the bone frame and use two spatulas to lift it onto a platter. Lift away the bone frame, gently turn the second fillet and scrape off the skin and the blood line as before. Arrange fillet on the platter beside the first piece.

To make the dressing, combine all the ingredients in a food processor and process to a creamy, spreadable consistency (add a little water if needed). Combine all the garnish ingredients in a bowl.

To serve, pour dressing over the fish and spread evenly. Coat thickly with the garnish mixture.

 This method of slow, enclosed cooking makes the fish fantastically tender.

SERVES 8–12

Moroccan grilled fish
with chermoula

2 teaspoons cumin seeds

2 cloves garlic, peeled

1 small onion, finely chopped

1 tablespoon chopped fresh
   coriander or flat-leaf parsley

2 teaspoons salt flakes

1 teaspoon ground sweet paprika

¼ teaspoon ground hot chilli

freshly ground black pepper

2 tablespoons olive oil

4 firm fish steaks (e.g. tuna)

To make the chermoula, first toast the cumin seeds in a dry small pan over medium heat until fragrant (about 1 minute), stirring occasionally. Tip into a spice grinder and crush. Now add the garlic, onion, coriander or parsley, salt, paprika, chilli and pepper. Grind to a paste, gradually adding the oil.

Spread mixture on both sides of the fish and set aside for 20 minutes to absorb flavours.

Preheat a barbecue, grill or heavy pan and brush very lightly with oil. Cook the fish over medium–high heat for 2½–3 minutes on each side, until cooked through.

Serve with a salad or couscous.

SERVES 4

Pan-fried fish
with crunchy dukkah coating

4 fish fillets (e.g. snapper, bream, dory)

salt and pepper

⅓ cup white rice crumbs or couscous

2 tablespoons dukkah (see note below)

2 tablespoons olive oil

1 tablespoon butter

freshly squeezed juice of 1 lemon

Season the fish fillets with salt and pepper. (If the fish is not moist enough to hold the crumbs, brush or spray with olive oil.) Combine rice crumbs and dukkah, and press onto both sides of the fish.

Heat the oil in a non-stick pan and fry the fish for 1½–2 minutes on each side, until cooked through. Remove to plates or a platter. Add the butter and lemon juice to the pan, heat to bubbling and then pour over the fish.

 Rice crumbs (available where gluten-free products are sold) or couscous make a good alternative to breadcrumbs. Dukkah is a Middle Eastern spice mixture that you'll find in delis and specialist food stores.

SERVES 4

Pepper-crusted tuna skewers with tzatziki

600–700 g tuna

1 tablespoon olive oil

salt

1½–2 tablespoons cracked
pepper (use a mix of pink,
green, white and black
peppercorns)

2–3 teaspoons chopped fresh
rosemary

1¼ cups Greek-style yoghurt

1½ tablespoons finely chopped
fresh mint, parsley or chives

½ cup grated (unpeeled)
cucumber

freshly squeezed lemon juice

extra salt and pepper

shredded lettuce

Cut the tuna into 2.5-cm cubes and coat lightly with olive oil and salt.
Thread onto eight skewers and sprinkle generously with the cracked
pepper and rosemary, pressing it on firmly. Set aside.

To make tzatziki, beat the yoghurt in a bowl and stir in the herbs and
cucumber. Add lemon juice, salt and pepper to taste.

Heat a grill or nonstick pan and cook the tuna skewers, turning to expose
every side to the heat, until the surface is crisp and the fish remains tender
inside (about 3 minutes). To serve, arrange two skewers on each plate over
shredded lettuce, spoon some tzatziki over, and serve.

SERVES 4

Rainbow trout with almonds

4 small whole trout, cleaned

½ cup milk

¾ cup plain flour seasoned with
salt and white pepper

200 g unsalted butter

¾ cup flaked or slivered
almonds

juice of 1 lemon

chopped fresh parsley,
dill or chives

Rinse trout in cold water, drain, and pat dry with paper towels. Make several diagonal slashes across both sides at the thicker end near the head. Dip trout in milk and then coat evenly with the seasoned flour, including the cavity.

Heat a large non-stick frying pan and add two-thirds of the butter.

Put in the fish and cook over medium heat for about 4 minutes on each side, until cooked through. Transfer to warmed plates. Increase the heat marginally, add remaining butter to the pan with the almonds. Fry until golden-brown, then add lemon juice, salt and pepper to taste, and the chopped herbs.

Spoon the sauce over the fish, and serve at once.

SERVES 4

Roulade of salmon stuffed with anchovies & tapenade

4 salmon fillets (or use tuna), about 150 g each

3 tablespoons bought tapenade

3 anchovy fillets in oil, drained and chopped

2 teaspoons chopped fresh basil

2 tablespoons fruity olive oil

Working from the thin end, slice horizontally through the salmon fillets without cutting right to the end. Open out lengthways, to form extra-long pieces.

Combine the tapenade, anchovies and basil with 1 tablespoon of the oil, and spread across one side of each piece of fish. Roll up, and secure with a couple of toothpicks.

Heat a non-stick pan on medium-high heat. Brush the fish roulades with the remaining oil and cook for about 2½ minutes on each side, or until cooked but still pink and tender in the middle.

Serve with a salad or grilled vegetables dressed with balsamic vinegar.

You can buy tapenade, an earthy Provençale purée of olives, capers and olive oil, at most good delis.

SERVES 4

Salmon cakes

400–450 g salmon fillets

3 spring onions (white and pale-green parts only), very finely chopped

grated zest of ½ lemon

2 tablespoons chopped fresh parsley or basil

1 cup soft fresh breadcrumbs

1 egg, beaten

salt and pepper

½ cup plain flour

½ cup light olive oil

Finely dice the salmon and place half in a food processor. Add half of the spring onions, lemon zest, parsley and breadcrumbs, and process to a paste. Combine this mixture with the remaining salmon and flavourings, stir in the egg, and season to taste with salt and pepper. Form into patties about 2 cm thick and coat with flour.

Heat the oil in a wide flat pan and fry the patties over medium heat for 2½ minutes on the first side and 1–2 minutes on the other side, until browned and cooked through.

 You can serve the salmon cakes as a stack, layered with small salad leaves and marinated red capsicum, dressed with a Thai-style sauce. Alternatively, serve with a salad of watercress and shredded carrot with a vinaigrette dressing that includes orange juice and grated orange zest.

MAKES 8

Sashimi of salmon
& King George whiting

⅓ cup dried wakame seaweed

1 × 180-g salmon steak

1 King George whiting fillet

1 spring onion

1 teaspoon sesame oil

1½ teaspoons rice vinegar

¼ cup tamari, soy sauce or ponzu sauce

1–2 teaspoons wasabi paste

½ lemon

Place the seaweed in a bowl and cover with boiling water. Set aside to expand, then transfer to iced water to chill.

Use a sharp knife to cut the salmon and whiting into slices 3 cm thick, cutting on the bias to ensure tenderness.

Slice the spring onion very finely and place in a small bowl. Cover with boiling water, leave for 10 seconds, then drain and refresh in cold water. Drain the soaked wakame and wrap, along with the drained spring onion, in paper towel to get rid of any excess water. Unwrap, transfer to a bowl and season with the sesame oil, rice vinegar and 1 teaspoon of the tamari, soy or ponzu sauce. ❯

Mound a portion of the wakame salad on each plate, and arrange the salmon and whiting on top. Place a dab of wasabi in small individual sauce dishes and place one on each plate. Serve the remaining tamari, soy or ponzu sauce in a small jug or bowl, for mixing with the wasabi.

Slice the lemon very finely and arrange a few slices on each plate.

Serve chilled.

If you don't care for raw fish, you can sear it before slicing. To do so, season with salt and pepper, rub with oil and cook each surface very briefly on a hot non-stick pan. Transfer fish to a dish of iced water to stop the cooking, and dry with paper towels before slicing.

SERVES 4 AS AN ENTRÉE

Seared salmon
with dill & lemon butter

2 salmon steaks

3 tablespoons unsalted butter

1 tablespoon chopped dill tips

½–1 lemon

sea salt flakes and freshly ground black pepper

To be at its best, salmon is seared but barely warmed inside, which produces crisped upper and lower surfaces, and about 7 mm of palest pink beneath, while the centre retains its bright original colour. You may, of course, cook the fish right through, but take care not to overcook or the result will be dry and unpalatable.

Heat a non-stick pan to medium–high and in it melt 1 tablespoon of the butter. Sear the salmon steaks for about 2 minutes on one side, then turn. After cooking them for about 1½ minutes on the other side (or until done to your taste), add the remaining butter, the dill tips, a big squeeze of lemon juice, and salt and pepper.

Allow the butter to bubble up, and then baste the salmon with it.

Serve the salmon over crisped noodles, spinach or mashed potatoes. (A lightly seasoned purée of steamed celeriac or cauliflower makes an excellent, less conventional accompaniment.)

SERVES 2

Seared tuna with avocado salsa

2 tuna steaks

salt and pepper

4 tablespoons avocado oil
  or light olive oil

1½ tablespoons lemon juice

4 cherry tomatoes

4 yellow grape tomatoes

½ small red onion, finely
  chopped

1 large ripe avocado, peeled
  and flesh cubed

2–3 tablespoons chopped fresh
  herbs (e.g. flat-leaf parsley,
  dill, coriander)

baby rocket leaves, to serve

Brush the tuna steaks with oil and season with salt and pepper. Heat a heavy, ribbed pan to very hot and put the steaks in to sear until darkly marked on the underside, then turn and cook the other side (total cooking time is 2–3 minutes, leaving the tuna pink inside). Set aside to rest.

Combine the remaining oil in a bowl with the lemon juice, and season with salt and pepper. Cut the cherry and grape tomatoes into quarters and add their juices to the dressing, reserving the flesh.

Place the onion in the bowl with the dressing, then add the avocado, tomatoes and chopped herbs, and mix lightly.

Spread rocket leaves on a serving plate. Thickly slice the tuna and arrange on the rocket, then spoon the avocado salsa over and serve.

SERVES 2 (3 AS AN ENTRÉE OR LIGHT LUNCH)

Smoked salmon dip

100 g smoked salmon

100 g cream cheese

½ cup sour cream

juice and zest of 1 lime or lemon

2 tablespoons white onion, very finely chopped

2 tablespoons dill tips, chopped

freshly ground black pepper

chilli sauce or Tabasco, to taste

Place three-quarters of the smoked salmon in a food processor with the cream cheese, sour cream and lime or lemon juice. Process for about 40 seconds, or until salmon is well chopped. Cut remaining salmon slices into small pieces and stir into the cream-cheese mixture with the lemon or lime zest, onion and dill. Season to taste with pepper and chilli or Tabasco sauce.

Spoon dip into a bowl, and serve with crisp bagel or pita chips, or with sourdough bread sliced thinly and oven-dried.

SERVES 8

Steamed fish with
spring vegetables & salsa verde

1 × 350-g thick piece reef fish
(e.g. coral trout) or flathead,
cut into 4

salt and pepper

sprigs of fresh dill or fennel

½ cup fresh basil or mint leaves

sprigs of fresh rosemary

4 baby carrots, trimmed

2 stems broccolini

1 × 4-cm piece daikon, peeled
and cut into 4

2 small spring onions, trimmed

4 small new potatoes

2 baby zucchinis

handful of snow peas

salsa verde (page 246)

Place fish pieces in the centre of a piece of oiled cling wrap. Sprinkle with salt and pepper, and place dill or fennel sprigs on top. Roll up, pierce all over with the point of a sharp knife, and set aside.

Place the basil or mint leaves and the rosemary sprigs in the bottom of a steamer and add about 4 cm of water. Bring to the boil, then arrange the vegetables in the steamer, cover and steam for about 6 minutes.

Push the vegetables aside and nestle the wrapped fish amongst them, then steam a further 6 minutes, or until the fish and vegetables are tender.

Unwrap the fish, serve surrounded by the steamed vegetables, and drizzle with salsa verde.

SERVES 2

Steamed rock cod
with ginger & shallots

1 × 1–1.4 kg rock cod or snapper

2 tablespoons oil

¼ cup light soy sauce

2 tablespoons rice wine or mirin

1 × 3-cm piece fresh ginger, thinly shredded

3 spring onions (use only the white parts and 5 cm of the greens)

Rinse the fish well, drain, and dry with paper towels. With a sharp knife, make regularly spaced diagonal slashes on each side, cutting down to the bone. Set the fish on a plate which will fit inside the steamer, and pour over it the oil, soy sauce and wine or mirin.

Cut the spring onions into 2.5-cm lengths, then shred lengthways. Scatter, with the ginger shreds, evenly over the fish, placing some in the cavity.

Set the steamer over high heat, add about 4 cm of water and bring to the boil, then reduce to a simmer. Place fish on its plate in the steamer, cover tightly and cook for about 15 minutes, or until the flesh is tender and easily flaked at its thickest part (just below the head). Serve the fish, on its plate, at the table.

SERVES 4–6 (MORE, IF SHARING SEVERAL DISHES)

Tapas of tuna with marinated capsicum & rocket pesto

1½ teaspoons crushed garlic

½ teaspoon freshly ground black pepper

2–3 tablespoons extra-virgin olive oil

2 × 2-cm-thick tuna steaks

2–3 slices ciabatta or sourdough bread

5–6 pieces marinated capsicum
(enough to fit the bread), well drained

rocket pesto (page 243)

Mix the garlic and pepper with the oil. Brush over both sides of the fish and on one side of each slice of bread.

Heat a ribbed pan over medium-high heat and grill the swordfish until the surface is well seared and fish is cooked through (about 2 minutes in total).

Grill the bread, oiled side down, then turn and grill the other surface. Cover the oiled surface with capsicum pieces, then place the swordfish on top.

Use a sharp knife to cut each slice into 2.5-cm squares. Top each with a teaspoon of rocket pesto, pierce with a toothpick, and serve.

MAKES ABOUT 24 PIECES

Tartlets of trout tartare

1 × 100-g trout (or salmon) fillet

1 tablespoon very finely chopped red onion

1 tablespoon very finely chopped fresh coriander leaves

2 teaspoons freshly squeezed lime juice

1 tablespoon finely chopped cucumber (deseed first)

2 tablespoons finely diced avocado

salt and pepper

3 teaspoons aioli (page 242)

a few drops of Tabasco or chilli sauce

18–20 small savoury pastry shells

18–20 small sprigs dill

Very finely chop the fish and mix with all the other ingredients except the dill sprigs. Place 1–1½ teaspoons of the mixture into each of the pastry shells, and decorate with a dill sprig. Serve within 20 minutes.

 Fish served raw must be super-fresh: try to find a supplier who specialises in fish for sashimi

MAKES 18–20

Tempura whiting
with ginger soy sauce

12 sand whiting fillets, or 4–6 King George whiting fillets

oil for deep-frying

2 egg yolks

2 cups iced water

2 cups sifted plain flour

extra flour, for coating

8 green beans, cut in half

4 spring onions, cut into 4-cm lengths
   (discard top greens)

GINGER SOY SAUCE

1½ tablespoons grated fresh ginger

½ cup light soy sauce

Check the fish for bones. Cut sand whiting fillets in half, or larger fillets into 5-cm pieces.

To make the sauce, simply combine the ingredients, squeezing the ginger to extract the juice.

Pour the oil into a wok or pan suitable for deep-frying and heat to 180°C.

Make the batter in two batches (it must be used very quickly once mixed), beginning with 1 egg yolk beaten lightly in a bowl. Add 1 cup of iced water and mix lightly, then add 1 cup of flour all at once and very, very lightly stir it into the liquid, leaving it lumpy. Do not overmix.

Have ready a rack over a tray lined with paper towels, for depositing the fried food. Place the remaining flour in a shallow dish.

When ready to begin cooking, dip each piece of fish first in flour (coat lightly, and shake off any excess), then into the batter and straight into the oil. Deep-fry until lightly golden (about 1 minute), retrieve with a slotted spoon or tongs, and set aside on the rack to drain.

When the first batter is used up, quickly mix another batch. Flour and batter the beans and spring onions in the same way as the fish, and fry for about 1 minute, until lightly golden. Arrange the cooked fish and vegetables on a platter or plates and serve hot, with the ginger soy sauce alongside for dipping.

 Oil for deep-frying should be heated to 170°–190°C. If you don't have a thermometer, drop a small cube of white bread into the oil: it should turn golden and float to the surface in 30 seconds. Alternatively, dip the handle end of a wooden spoon in the centre of the pan: if a cloud of tiny bubbles forms around the handle, the oil is ready.

SERVES 4

Teriyaki fish with
wakame & cucumber salad

4 mackerel steaks

salt

2 tablespoons oil

3 tablespoons sake

3 tablespoons mirin

3 tablespoons dark soy sauce

1½ teaspoons sugar

sesame seeds

steamed white rice, to serve

WAKAME & CUCUMBER SALAD

½ cup dried wakame

2 Lebanese cucumbers

2 teaspoons sesame oil

1 tablespoon light olive oil
   or vegetable oil

2 tablespoons rice vinegar

1 teaspoon sugar

2 teaspoons sesame seeds,
   for garnish

To make the salad, first soak wakame in warm water until it expands, then drain thoroughly and shred. Use a vegetable peeler to shave the unpeeled cucumber into ribbons, and mix these with the wakame. Combine the oil, rice vinegar and sugar, and pour over the salad. Toast sesame seeds in a dry pan until golden, and sprinkle over the salad. Set aside until required.

To cook the fish, sprinkle both sides of each steak with salt and set aside for 20 minutes before cooking.

Heat the oil in a heavy iron or non-stick pan. Fry the fish over high heat until the underside is well browned (about 2½ minutes), then turn and cook the other side for about 1 minute. ❯

Lift fish out and place on a wire rack over the sink. Carefully pour boiling water over the fish to remove excess oil, and when drained return to the hot pan with the sake, mirin, soy sauce and sugar. Baste the fish continually until the sauce is reduced to a rich glossy glaze.

Carefully lift cooked fish onto warmed plates, spooning any remaining sauce over, and sprinkle with sesame seeds. Serve with steamed white rice and the crunchy salad.

SERVES 4

Thai crispy snapper with sweet chilli sauce

1 whole snapper (about 1.2 kg)

1 teaspoon salt

1 cup cornflour

oil for deep-frying

SAUCE

½ cup sweet chilli sauce

1 cup water

3½ teaspoons cornflour

freshly squeezed lime juice
   to taste

fish sauce to taste

black pepper

sugar (optional)

Rinse the fish, drain well and pat dry with paper towels. Make a series of deep, diagonal slashes along each side, season with salt and set aside for a few minutes.

Meanwhile, make the sauce by combining the sweet chilli sauce, water and cornflour in a saucepan. Bring to the boil, stirring, and simmer for about 1½ minutes until the sauce thickens and clears. Add a squeeze of lime juice, a few drops of fish sauce and some freshly ground black pepper to taste (plus a little sugar to soften the chilli bite, if you like).

Drain the fish and pat dry with paper towels. Coat with the cornflour, brushing it into the slashes.

Heat a large pan of oil to very hot, carefully slide in the fish and fry until golden and crisp. Use a ladle to baste the fish constantly with the oil   ❯

while cooking, and turn once or twice. Lift the fish out carefully, drain, and place on a platter (see note below). Pour the sauce over, and serve at once (or you can add the sauce at the table).

The fish looks sensational when served standing upright on a platter. To do so, spread open the body cavity so the pectoral fins form legs, and balance the fish on these, propping it upright with lime halves and sprigs of basil if necessary.

Thai fish cakes

350 g firm fish fillets
(e.g. snapper, perch)

1 tablespoon fish sauce

1½ teaspoons red curry paste

salt and pepper

1 egg white

½ teaspoon baking powder

2 green beans, cut into paper-
thin slices

2–3 kaffir lime leaves, *very* finely
chopped

oil for deep-frying

chilli lime sauce (page 234)
or Vietnamese dipping sauce
(page 250)

Cut the fish into cubes and place in a food processor with fish sauce, curry paste, salt and pepper. Grind to a smooth purée, gradually adding the egg white and baking powder. (Add 1–2 tablespoons water if the mixture is stiff.)

When fish mixture is very smooth, stir in the beans and the lime leaves. With wet hands, shape into 18 small, flat cakes.

Heat oil in a wok or pan suitable for deep-frying until medium-hot. Fry the fish cakes in batches until golden, puffy and cooked through (about 3 minutes). Retrieve with a slotted spoon, and drain.

Serve with either (or both) of the dipping sauces.

MAKES 18

Tuna salad niçoise

2 tuna steaks

1½ cups sliced green beans

4 firm roma tomatoes,
  quartered

4 hard-boiled eggs, quartered

1 yellow or red capsicum, cut
  into 2-cm squares

1 red onion, sliced

8 anchovy fillets in oil,
  drained and chopped

18 kalamata olives

DRESSING

⅓ cup fruity extra-virgin
  olive oil

1½ tablespoons lemon juice
  or white wine vinegar

2 teaspoons Dijon mustard

salt and pepper

Steam or grill the tuna. Parboil beans in lightly salted water for 2 minutes, drain, refresh in cold water and then drain again.

Gently combine all the salad ingredients in a bowl.

To make the dressing, simply whisk together the oil, vinegar and mustard to make a creamy emulsion. Season to taste, drizzle over the salad, and serve.

You can substitite 1 × 425-g can tuna in oil for the fresh tuna. If so, simply drain and then separate tuna into chunks before combining with the other ingredients.

SERVES 4–6

Whole baked flounder
with herbs & lemon

2 whole flounder, cleaned

salt and pepper

2 sprigs each of sage, parsley, lemon thyme and basil

2 lemons, sliced thinly

2 tablespoons light olive oil

2 tablespoons butter

Preheat oven to 190°C.

Make 2–3 slashes on the upper side of each fish. Season the cavity with salt and pepper, and stuff with the herbs and one or two lemon slices.

Brush the bottom of a roasting pan with olive oil and put in the fish. Season the top lightly with salt and pepper and spread remaining lemon slices over. Dot fish with cubes of butter, then bake in preheated oven for about 15 minutes. Check fish after 10 minutes, and every 2 minutes after that, by pushing the point of a knife into the thickest part, near the head: when the knife goes in cleanly, the fish is done.

Serve fish on large plates. (The top skin can be carefully lifted off before serving, if you prefer.) Baby potatoes, steamed or boiled and then tossed with herbs and butter, are the perfect accompaniment.

SERVES 2

Seafood plus

Just about every seaboard country and cuisine features dishes in which a variety of seafood is used. In addition, seafood has traditionally been eked out with staples such as pasta, rice and other grains, starchy vegetables, and eggs.

When using a mixture of seafood in one dish, it's worth choosing it yourself so you know what you're getting and that the balance is right. Ready-made 'marinara' mixes contain very differing proportions of fish and shellfish: if you opt for this solution, do buy from a reliable fishmonger as the quality will always be better. And remember to allow for the different cooking requirements of seafoods when combining them in one dish: shellfish need only about 5 minutes; chunky fillets and steaks about 10 minutes in total; squid is best cooked fast, so it should be added towards the end.

< An elegant salmon & prawn mousse (page 84)

An elegant salmon & prawn mousse

300 g salmon fillets

2 tablespoons gelatine powder (or use 5½ × 5-g sheets)

2 spring onions, finely chopped

1 cup cream

200 g medium-sized cooked prawns, peeled

2 tablespoons chopped fresh parsley

zest and freshly squeezed juice of ½ lemon and 1 lime

1 tablespoon sweet chilli sauce

salt and white pepper

Poach the salmon in lightly salted water until just cooked. Transfer to a food processor, reserving the poaching water. Strain 1 cup of the water into a clean saucepan, set over low heat, add the gelatine and bring to the boil, stirring until clear.

Add the spring onions, the cream and half the prawns to the food processor, and process to a smooth paste.

Arrange the remaining prawns and the chopped parsley on the base of a wet mould, and cover with a thin layer of the gelatine mixture. Place in the freezer to set the mixture quickly.

Stir the remaining gelatine into the processed salmon mixture, adding half the lime and lemon zest, and lime and lemon juice to taste. Season with the sweet chilli sauce and the salt and pepper

Spread this mixture over the prawn jelly, cover with cling wrap, and chill until set.

To serve, unmould mousse onto a platter and garnish with the remaining lemon and lime zest. Accompany with a salad of small leaves tossed with a citrus vinaigrette.

SERVES 8–12 AS AN ENTRÉE (6 AS A MAIN DISH)

Angel-hair pasta
with scallops & saffron

180 g dried angel-hair pasta
  (or 250 g fresh)

¾ cup cream

a pinch of saffron threads

3 tablespoons butter

6–8 large scallops, roe left on

1 tablespoon finely chopped
  onion

½ teaspoon crushed garlic

salt and freshly ground pepper

chopped fresh chives, dill
  or basil

lemon wedges

Boil dried pasta in salted water for about 7 minutes, or fresh pasta for about 2 minutes. Tip into a colander to drain, and set aside.

Heat the cream almost to boiling in a microwave or small saucepan, add the saffron, and then set aside.

Melt 2 tablespoons of the butter in a small frying pan and when it's bubbling add the scallops and onion. Cook the scallops for about 2 minutes on the first side, then turn, add the garlic and continue cooking until the scallops are just firm and the onion is golden (about 1 minute more).

Set the scallops aside on a plate. ❯

Pour the saffron cream into the pan with the onion and add the remaining butter. Simmer until the sauce is glossy, then stir in the pasta and scallops and warm through, adding salt and pepper to taste.

Serve on warmed plates, garnished with the chopped herbs and a lemon wedge.

SERVES 2

Aussie mixed grill
of barramundi, bugs & prawns

2 barramundi steaks or fillets

2–3 teaspoons olive oil

sea salt flakes and native 'bush' pepper or black pepper

2 Balmain or Moreton Bay bugs

1 clove garlic, crushed

olive oil spray

4 large green (raw) prawns, shelled or unshelled as preferred

3 tablespoons unsalted butter

1½ tablespoons chopped mixed herbs (e.g. parsley, thyme, oregano, basil)

1 lemon, quartered

Pat the fish dry with paper towels and brush lightly with olive oil. Season with a sprinkle of salt flakes and pepper.

Cut the bugs in half, season lightly with salt and pepper, smear with crushed garlic and spray with olive oil. Also spray the prawns with olive oil.

Heat a heavy pan or barbecue and grill the prawns and bugs, cut surfaces down, for 3–4 minutes or until pink and firm, turning the prawns once or twice. Set aside and keep warm.

Heat a non-stick pan over medium heat, add 1½ tablespoons of the butter and when bubbling add the barramundi. Cook for 3 minutes on one side, then turn and cook the other side for 2–3 minutes, until fish feels firm and flakes when tested with a fork. Transfer to plates and arrange the grilled bugs and prawns on top. ➤

Add remaining butter to the pan and when it's sizzling add the herbs and a squeeze of lemon juice. Pour sauce over the seafood and serve at once, with one or two lemon quarters for squeezing.

SERVES 2

Bouillabaisse (seafood soup) with saffron rouille & parmesan crisps

2 fish carcases, including heads

6 large green (raw) prawns, shelled and deveined (reserve shells and head for stock)

1 large onion, quartered

1 tablespoon olive oil

2 cloves garlic, finely chopped

2 strips orange zest

1 cup tomato and basil pasta sauce, or diced fresh tomato

500 g fish fillets (e.g. snapper, flake, perch, flathead) cut into 2-cm cubes

12 mussels in their shells, cleaned

4 small cleaned squid, tubes cut into rings, and tentacles retained

salt and pepper

rouille (page 245)

parmesan toasts (see note page 93)

Rinse and drain the fish heads and carcases, and place in a large saucepan with the prawn shells and heads, half the onion, and cold water to cover. Bring slowly to the boil, then reduce heat and simmer very gently for about 20 minutes, skimming any froth or residue from the surface. Strain, and measure 7 cups.

Slice the remaining onion and sauté in the olive oil until softened (about 3 minutes).

Add the garlic, sauté briefly before adding the orange peel, pasta sauce or diced tomato, and the 7 cups of stock. Bring barely to the boil, reduce to a simmer and cook for 4–5 minutes. (At this stage the soup can be set aside until almost ready to serve. It takes just a few minutes to cook the seafood.)

Add the fish, prawns and mussels, salt and pepper to taste. Cover, and simmer for about 5 minutes or until seafood is tender. Finally, add the squid and cook briefly.

Serve in soup bowls, each on a plate accompanied by a small dish of rouille and a parmesan toast or two.

To make parmesan crisps, thinly slice a French bread stick and toast the slices on one side. Turn, cover the other side with grated parmesan, and toast under a hot grill until the bread is crisp and the cheese melted and browned.

SERVES 6–8

Chilled soba noodles with prawns & fish cake in soy sesame dressing

250 g soba (buckwheat) noodles

½ cup dashi stock

2 tablespoons dark soy sauce

2 tablespoons mirin

½ teaspoon sugar

2 tablespoons sesame oil

2 spring onions, very finely sliced

12 medium-sized raw (green) prawns in their shells

60 g Japanese fish cake (or use frozen fish balls, thawed)

chopped fresh coriander

Bring a saucepan of lightly salted water to the boil and cook the noodles for about 3 minutes. Drain, and rinse in cold water to remove excess starch. Leave in a colander to drain.

For the dressing, combine the dashi, soy sauce, mirin and sugar, and heat barely to boiling, then set aside to cool. When cold, add the sesame oil and spring onions.

In a steamer, cook the prawns and fish cake (or fish balls) for about 5 minutes, then remove and allow to cool. Shell and devein the prawns, and slice the fish cake (if using fish balls, cut in half).

In a mixing bowl combine the noodles with the seafood, sauce and coriander, mixing well. Serve in little glass bowls.

SERVES 4

Creamy curried pumpkin & prawn soup

20 medium-sized raw (green) prawns

½ cup finely diced onion

1½ tablespoons olive oil or butter

750 g pumpkin, peeled and cut into 1-cm cubes

1 tablespoon mild curry powder

salt and pepper

¾ cup sour cream or natural yoghurt

freshly squeezed juice of 1 lemon or lime

Shell the prawns and place the shells in a saucepan with water to cover, bring to boil and simmer for 15 minutes, then set aside.

In another saucepan gently cook the onion in the oil or butter until soft but not coloured (about 3 minutes). Add the pumpkin, curry powder and ½ cup water, and cover tightly. Cook over low heat, shaking the pan occasionally, until the pumpkin is almost tender (about 10 minutes).

Strain the prawn liquid, add 2 cups to the pan, add salt and pepper, and simmer until the pumpkin has collapsed. Whiz in a blender or food processor, or purée with a stick mixer. Devein the prawns and add to the soup. Simmer for about 6 minutes, until prawns are pink and tender, then stir in the sour cream or yoghurt, and add lemon or lime juice to taste.

SERVES 4

Crisp pizza with prawns, tomato & artichokes

2 thin-crust 18-cm pizza bases

2 teaspoons crushed garlic

200 ml tomato and basil
  pasta sauce

100 g grated mozzarella cheese
  (or use bocconcini, torn)

10 cherry tomatoes, sliced

¼ cup roasted capsicum in oil,
  diced

¼ cup roasted artichokes
  in oil, diced

12–16 medium-sized cooked
  prawns, shelled and deveined

salt and pepper

dried chilli flakes

salsa verde (page 246) or chopped
  fresh basil or coriander

Preheat oven to 200°C.

Spread garlic and pasta sauce over the pizza bases and scatter with the mozzarella. Arrange tomato slices, diced capsicum and artichokes, and prawns evenly on pizza bases. Season with salt and pepper and add a sprinkle of chilli flakes.

Bake in preheated oven for 12–15 minutes, until the cheese is bubbling and the crust crisp. Drizzle with salsa verde or sprinkle with herbs, and serve at once.

SERVES 2

Eggs benedict with smoked salmon

1 teaspoon white vinegar

4 eggs

2 English muffins

8 slices smoked salmon

chopped fresh chives or dill

HOLLANDAISE SAUCE

3 large egg yolks

1 tablespoon lemon juice

2 teaspoons white wine vinegar

180 g butter, cut into small cubes

To make the hollandaise sauce, first one-third fill a saucepan (or the base of a double saucepan) with water and bring to a simmer. In a bowl, or the top of the double saucepan, whisk the egg yolks, lemon juice, vinegar and 1 tablespoon water until combined.

Place bowl over the saucepan and continue whisking over heat until thick and foamy (about 1½ minutes – do not let the bowl touch the simmering water, or the eggs will begin to cook). Slowly whisk in the cubes of butter, whisking well until the sauce is thick and creamy. Remove the bowl from the heat and set aside.

To poach the eggs, bring a saucepan of water to the boil and add the vinegar. Break one of the eggs into a small dish. Stir the boiling water until it swirls, and then slide in the egg. When it has begun to set, add another egg and poach them for about 3 minutes, until the whites are firm and the yolk soft. Transfer to a bowl of hot water and set aside while you cook the remaining eggs in the same way. >

Split and toast the muffins, butter lightly and place two slices of smoked salmon on each half. Lift out the poached eggs, one at a time, and drain on a tea-towel. Nestle one on each prepared muffin, then top with hollandaise sauce and sprinkle with the chives or dill. Serve at once.

SERVES 4

Fettuccine with prawns, fennel & fresh tomato sauce

400 g fettuccine

salt

3 tablespoons olive oil

1 small bulb fennel (or use 1½ celery stalks and ⅓ teaspoon fennel seeds), chopped

20–24 raw (green) prawns, shelled and deveined

1 punnet cherry tomatoes, cut in half

1 tablespoon crushed dill seeds or 2 tablespoons chopped fresh herbs

4 tablespoons grated parmesan cheese (optional)

Bring 3 litres of water to the boil and add 2 teaspoons of salt. Add the fettuccine and simmer for 12 minutes or until al dente. When the pasta is half-cooked, heat the olive oil in a large frying pan and sauté the fennel (or celery sticks and fennel seeds) until softened (about 5 minutes).

Add the prawns and cook until they are just pink and firm (about 3 minutes). Add the tomatoes and cook for about 2 minutes, until tomatoes collapse and prawns are cooked through.

Drain the pasta and transfer to the prawn pan, adding herbs and parmesan (if using). Mix well and serve on warmed plates.

SERVES 4

Fritto misto
(a classic seafood basket)

12 prawn cutlets

12 fresh scallops, roe on

3 fish fillets (e.g. flatbead), cut
   lengthways into 6 thick strips,
   or use 12 sand whiting fillets

12 calamari rings

12 large oysters

meat from 12 mussels
   (or use grilled spicy
   mussels, page 205)

oil for deep-frying

crunchy potato chips (page 235)

lemon wedges and/or cider
   vinegar

1 cup tartare sauce (page 248)

CRUMB COATING

1½–2 cups plain flour

3 cups fine dry breadcrumbs

3–4 eggs, beaten with
   2 tablespoons milk

Pat the seafood dry with paper towels.

For the crumb coating, spread the flour and crumbs on separate flat plates, and place the egg-milk mixture in a shallow dish. Coat seafood lightly with flour, shaking off any excess, then dip into the egg, allowing excess to drip off before placing in crumbs. Then coat lightly but evenly with crumbs. Spread the crumbed pieces on trays and refrigerate for at least 1 hour before frying. (This helps to set the crumbs and create a sealed coating, which crisps well in the oil.)

When ready to cook, heat the oil to 170–190°C in a pan suitable for deep-frying. Set a cake rack over a tray lined with paper towels, for draining the cooked seafood. Depending on the size of the pan and the amount of oil, fry only 6–10 pieces at a time, to avoid overcrowding the pan (which cools the frying oil, and excess oil is absorbed into the crumb coating). Fry prawns for 2–4 minutes, scallops for 2–3 minutes, fish for 3–6 minutes, and calamari, oysters and mussels for ½–1 minute.

Pile cooked seafood onto a large platter with potato chips, lemon wedges (for squeezing) or vinegar, salt and the tartare sauce.

Instead of breadcrumbs you can use Japanese panko crumbs, which give a lighter, crisper result. They are available from Asian food stores and some delis. Rice crumbs or fine polenta are good gluten-free alternatives.

SERVES 6

Gazpacho with seafood

¾ cup finely diced tomato

¾ cup finely diced cucumber

1 cup diced red capsicum

1 cup diced yellow or green
   capsicum

½ cup finely diced red onion

1 clove garlic, chopped

juice of ½ lemon

salt and pepper

1½ tablespoons red wine vinegar

2 tablespoons fruity olive oil
   (optional)

½ cup cooked and peeled small
   prawns (or large cooked
   prawns, chopped)

½ cup flaked crab meat

2 anchovies in oil, drained
   and chopped

chopped fresh coriander, and
   diced avocado, for garnish

lemon wedges

Combine the vegetables in a bowl and add the garlic and lemon juice, with salt and pepper to taste. Mix well, cover and chill for several hours.

Transfer three-quarters of the vegetables to a food processor and chop coarsely. Stir back into the diced vegetables and add enough iced water, with the vinegar and olive oil (if using), to achieve desired texture.

Spoon gazpacho into chilled bowls. Divide the prawns, crab meat and anchovies between the bowls, and garnish with the coriander and avocado. Serve with lemon wedges alongside.

SERVES 6–8

Linguine with trout
& asparagus in cream sauce

200 g linguine

salt

8 asparagus stems, trimmed and
  cut in half

1 trout fillet (about 180 g)

1 tablespoon olive oil

1 small clove garlic, crushed

1 × 10-cm piece of spring onion
  white, very finely chopped

¼ cup dry white wine

½ cup sour cream

black pepper

chopped fresh dill, mint
  or parsley

Bring 1.5 litres of water to the boil and add 1½ teaspoons salt. Add the linguine and cook for 9–10 minutes, until barely al dente.

Add the asparagus to the saucepan and boil for another 2 minutes, then drain and set aside.

In a small frying pan, heat the oil to hot. Brush the fish with oil and cook for about 2½ minutes on the first side, then turn and cook for another 2 minutes, or until done to taste (ideally still pink on the inside). Remove to a plate.

Add remaining oil to the pan and add the garlic and spring onion. Sauté for 1 minute, then deglaze the pan with the wine, simmering until it has almost evaporated. Add sour cream and simmer briefly.   >

Break the fish into cubes. Warm the linguine and asparagus in the sauce and then add the fish, salt and black pepper, and chopped herbs. Mix gently together, and serve on warmed plates or wide shallow bowls.

SERVES 2

Lobster finger sandwiches

6 slices white sandwich bread

12 slices wholemeal
  sandwich bread

softened butter

280 g lobster meat

4 tablespoons mayonnaise

3 tablespoons soft cream cheese

squeeze of lemon juice

2 Lebanese cucumbers,
  sliced paper-thin

salt and pepper

finely shredded iceberg lettuce,
  to serve

Lightly butter the bread on one side.

In a bowl, shred the lobster meat with your fingers. Add mayonnaise, cream cheese and lemon juice, mixing well.

Spread filling evenly over the white bread slices and top each with a wholemeal slice. Turn over and butter the exposed white bread, then cover with cucumber and season with salt and pepper. Top with a wholemeal slice, and gently press with a spatula or egg flip.

With a very sharp serrated knife, remove crusts and cut each sandwich into two or three fingers. Arrange over shredded lettuce and serve at once.

MAKES 12 OR 18

Paella

3 tablespoons extra-virgin olive oil

1 medium-sized onion, finely chopped

2 cloves garlic, crushed

2 cups paella rice (calasparra or bomba: see note page 112) or medium-grain rice

1 × 400-g can crushed tomatoes

3½ cups fish stock

1½ teaspoons saffron threads

2 teaspoons ground sweet paprika

16 medium-sized green (raw) prawns, shelled but tails left on

300 g white fish fillets, cut into 2-cm cubes

2 large squid tubes, sliced into rings

12 mussels in their shells

¾ cup frozen peas

chopped fresh parsley

Heat the oil in a paella pan and fry the onion over on medium-low heat for 3 minutes, until softened and lightly coloured. Add the garlic and fry briefly.

Pour the rice into the pan and stir until coated with the oil, then add the tomatoes and two cups of the stock. Simmer, stirring occasionally, until the rice is half cooked (about 12 minutes).

Add the saffron, paprika and prawns, and another cup of stock. Cook for 2–3 minutes, then add the fish, squid, mussels and peas, with salt and pepper to taste. Cook gently, stirring occasionally but without disturbing ❯

the contents of the pan unnecessarily, until the rice is tender and the seafood cooked (about 3 minutes).

Scatter with plenty of chopped parsley before serving from the pan.

Rice for paella should be medium-grain. You can find Spanish calasparra and bomba rice in specialist food stores. Otherwise, use any good-quality medium-grain rice, including Italian arborio (used for risotto).

SERVES 4

Pasta with mussels, green beans & pesto

400 g spaghetti or other pasta

12 green beans, topped, tailed and cut into 3 pieces

28 mussels in their shells

basil, rocket or coriander pesto (page 243)

½ lemon or lime (optional)

shaved parmesan cheese, for garnish

Bring 2 litres of water to the boil and add 1½ teaspoons salt. Boil the pasta until al dente (9–12 minutes, depending on type of pasta). Add the beans for the last 2 minutes. Drain and set aside.

Steam the mussels open in about ½ cup white wine (this can be done ahead) and remove meat from shells. Reserve the cooking liquid and place in large pan.

Add the pasta, beans and mussels to the pan with a generous amount of pesto, and toss over medium heat until well mixed. Serve garnished with parmesan.

SERVES 4

Prawn cannelloni with tomato & cheese sauce

6 tablespoons butter

3 tablespoons very finely chopped onion

4 tablespoons flour

3 cups milk

salt and pepper

140 g cooked prawn meat, finely chopped

1 tablespoon chopped fresh parsley or basil

8 instant cannelloni tubes

5 teaspoons tomato paste

$\frac{1}{3}$ teaspoon chicken stock powder

$\frac{1}{3}$ teaspoon ground or freshly grated nutmeg

$\frac{1}{2}$ cup grated parmesan cheese

Preheat the oven to 180°C.

Heat half the butter in a small pan and sauté the onion over medium heat for about 2½ minutes, until softened. Stir in half the flour and cook, stirring with a wooden spoon, for about 1 minute. Add 1 cup of milk and stir or whisk until smooth, then add another ½ cup milk and a little salt and pepper, and simmer, stirring slowly, until it comes to the boil and becomes quite thick. Add the prawns and herbs, and simmer briefly.

Spoon or pipe the prawn mixture into the cannelloni tubes and arrange them side by side in a well greased dish. Mix the tomato paste with 1 cup water and pour over the cannelloni. ❯

In a clean saucepan, melt the remaining 3 tablespoons of butter and when bubbling stir in the remaining 2 tablespoons of flour with a wooden spoon. Cook, stirring slowly, for about 1 minute, then add the remaining milk, the chicken stock powder, nutmeg and a little salt and pepper, and simmer, whisking gently, until thickened.

Carefully spoon this sauce over the cannelloni, covering the tomato liquid. Scatter the parmesan evenly on top and bake in preheated oven for about 30 minutes, until the top is golden and bubbling and the cannelloni tender.

SERVES 3–4

Prosciutto-wrapped prawn & fish skewers

½ teaspoon crushed garlic

½ teaspoon ground cumin

½ teaspoon salt flakes

⅓ teaspoon freshly ground black pepper

3 teaspoons chopped fresh coriander or basil

3 teaspoons chopped fresh parsley

½ teaspoon finely chopped fresh rosemary

2 tablespoons olive oil

8 large green (raw) prawns, shelled and deveined

200 g firm-textured fish (e.g. mackerel or tuna), cut into 8 cubes

16 large, very thin slices of prosciutto

1 red capsicum, cut into 2-cm squares

white parts of 2 spring onions, cut into 2-cm lengths

salad, to serve

You will need 8 metal or bamboo skewers: if using bamboo, soak in cold water for 10 minutes before using, to prevent them burning.

In a bowl combine the garlic, cumin, salt, pepper and half the herbs, with the oil. Add the seafood and stir to coat evenly. Cover with plastic wrap, and refrigerate for several hours, turning occasionally.

Preheat barbecue or grill to medium–hot.   >

Cut the prosciutto slices in half lengthways. Wrap each prawn with 3 strips of prosciutto, and each fish cube with 1 strip. Thread onto the skewers, alternating the seafood with pieces of capsicum and spring onion.

Brush the prepared skewers with some of the remaining marinade. Cook on the preheated barbecue or grill, turning several times, until done (5–7 minutes).

Serve with salad or a fruity couscous (see note below).

To make a fruity couscous that goes well with these skewers, first soften couscous in boiling stock or water. Fluff with a fork, add butter, salt and pepper, chopped fresh herbs and finely diced fruit such as pineapple, mango and nashi pear.

SERVES 4

Salad of marinated mussels with olives & tomatoes

1 cup bought marinated mussels

1½ cups sliced green beans

1 red onion, chopped

¾ cup mixed marinated olives

¾ cup semi-dried tomatoes, halved

3 roma tomatoes, sliced

¼ cup extra-virgin olive oil

1 tablespoon red wine vinegar

salt to taste

½ cup tomato and herb pasta sauce

½ cup chopped fresh parsley

2 tablespoons chopped fresh basil

a little chopped fresh red chilli

freshly ground black pepper

sugar to taste (optional)

Drain the mussels and place in a bowl.

Boil the beans for 5 minutes, or until tender but with a little bite, then drain. Add beans, onion, and semi-dried and fresh tomatoes to the mussels and mix well.

In another bowl, make a simple dressing by whisking together the olive oil, vinegar and salt. Combine with the tomato pasta sauce, parsley, basil and chilli, and pour over the salad. Season to taste with salt and pepper, and a pinch of sugar if needed, and toss thoroughly.

SERVES 4–6

Salmon sushi rolls

1 cup sushi rice or medium-grain white rice

2 tablespoons sushi seasoning (see note page 123)

3 sheets nori (compressed seaweed)

90–120 g smoked or fresh salmon, cut into thin strips

3–4 cos lettuce leaves, finely shredded

1½ tablespoons Japanese pickled ginger

1–2 teaspoons wasabi paste

tamari or light soy sauce, to serve

Place rice in a small saucepan with 1¾ cups water. Cover tightly and bring to the boil. Reduce heat, and simmer (without removing the lid), for about 12 minutes, until water is absorbed and rice tender. While rice is still warm, stir sushi seasoning through, using a wide spoon, and spread in a shallow dish to cool.

Light a gas flame or heat a hotplate, and briefly hold each nori sheet over the heat to make pliable (about 15 seconds).

Place one sheet of nori on a sushi mat or bamboo place mat. With wet hands, spread the nori with rice, leaving 2 cm uncovered at the top and bottom. Arrange salmon strips, lettuce and pickled ginger slices along the centre of the rice and add a few dots of wasabi. Fold the bottom edge of ❯

the mat up over the sushi and squeeze gently to form a cylinder, then roll up. Prepare the other two sushi rolls in the same way.

With a very sharp knife cut each roll into 6–8 pieces. Serve with any remaining pickled ginger and wasabi paste, and the soy sauce for dipping.

You can buy ready-made sushi seasoning at Asian food stores. To make your own, simply mix 1½ tablespoons rice vinegar with 1 teaspoon sugar and ½ teaspoon salt.

MAKES 18–24

Sand-crab lasagne

2½ tablespoons olive oil

275 g fresh (or use frozen) crab meat

4 spring onions (use white parts and 4 cm of green only), chopped

1 clove garlic, crushed

2 teaspoons mirin or dry sherry

1 tablespoon fish sauce (or 2 mashed anchovies)

1 cup fish stock

2 eggs, separated

3 teaspoons cornflour

chopped fresh coriander or dill

2 tablespoons sour cream

12 fresh lasagne sheets

extra, fruity olive oil

extra chopped fresh herbs (e.g. basil, dill)

Flake crab meat and pick out any scraps of shell. Heat the oil in a frying pan and gently sauté the spring onions and garlic for 2 minutes. Add the mirin or sherry, cook for 20 seconds and then add the crab meat and stir to warm through.

Stir the fish sauce into the fish stock and add to the pan, stirring until stock comes to the boil.

Whisk the egg whites until just broken up. Remove crab mixture from the heat and drizzle in the egg white using a fork, allowing it to set in fine strings. Stir the cornflour into 2 tablespoons cold water, then stir into the

>

crab mixture and cook for 30 seconds until thickened, stir in a sprinkle of chopped coriander or dill, the egg yolks and the sour cream.

Bring a pan of salted water to the boil and cook lasagne sheets for about 2–3 minutes, or until just tender. Drain well, and pat dry before using.

Place a lasagne sheet on each plate, top with a spoonful of the crab filling, then repeat layers (ending with a lasagne sheet). Finish with a generous drizzle of fruity olive oil, and a scattering of the extra chopped herbs.

SERVES 4

Scallop & green-pea risotto

1.5 litres fish stock

500 g scallops, roe left on

100 g unsalted butter

sea salt and cracked black pepper

1 small onion, finely chopped

500 g arborio or other
   risotto rice

200 ml dry white wine

a large pinch of saffron threads

1–2 cups fresh green peas, boiled
   for 1 minute and then drained

2 tablespoons finely chopped
   fresh parsley

extra salt and pepper

Heat the stock in a saucepan, and keep warm.

Separate the roe from the scallop meat (if the scallops are large, cut them in half). Heat half the butter in a small frying pan and quickly sauté the white parts of the scallops, turning once. Season to taste with salt and pepper, then tip into a bowl.

Reheat the pan with the remaining butter and sauté the onion over medium-low heat until soft. Add the rice and stir until each grain is coated with the butter and the rice is hot. Add the wine and sizzle until it evaporates. Now slowly add the stock, a ladleful at a time, stirring slowly and allowing the rice to absorb the liquid before adding more. After a few ladlefuls, add the saffron threads and stir through the rice.

When the rice is about three-quarters cooked (about 15 minutes), add the peas, the cooked scallop whites with their cooking liquid, the roe and the ❯

parsley. Season to taste, and continue to cook, adding more stock as needed, until the risotto is creamy and each grain is soft on the outside and firm inside.

Serve in large shallow bowls.

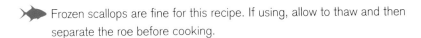 Frozen scallops are fine for this recipe. If using, allow to thaw and then separate the roe before cooking.

SERVES 6–8

Seafood & celery salad in a creamy dressing

12 medium-sized cooked
   prawns, peeled

½ cup crab meat, flaked

12 bought marinated mussels

2 slices smoked salmon, cut into
   strips

3 celery sticks, diagonally sliced

2 spring onions, finely sliced

2 tablespoons chopped fresh
   parsley, basil or mint

1–2 tablespoons sour cream

3–4 tablespoons mayonnaise
   (page 242)

soft lettuce leaves (e.g.
   mignonette), shredded

Combine the seafood, celery, spring onions and herbs in a bowl.

Whisk the sour cream and mayonnaise together until smooth, pour over the salad and mix well. Serve over shredded lettuce.

SERVES 4

Seafood omelette, Asian-style

80 g crab meat

80 g small shelled prawns
(or diced scallops)

⅓ cup frozen peas, thawed (or
6 fresh snow peas, cut in half)

1 tablespoon vegetable oil

2 spring onions, chopped
(keep white and green
parts separate)

¾ cup fish stock

1½ teaspoons rice wine

salt and white pepper

1½ teaspoons cornflour

4 eggs, separated

1 teaspoon sesame oil

oyster sauce, to serve

Pick over crab meat and prawns (if using) to remove any fragments of shell.

Blanch snow peas (if using) in boiling water for 1 minute, then drain and set aside.

In a small pan heat half the vegetable oil and sauté the white parts of the spring onions for 40 seconds. Add the crab meat, prawns or scallops, peas or snow peas, fish stock, rice wine, salt and pepper and simmer for 2–3 minutes.

Mix the cornflour into 2 tablespoons of water, then stir into the seafood mixture until thickened and translucent (about 40 seconds). Remove mixture from heat and then set aside, keeping warm.   ❯

Beat the egg yolks and 2 of the whites with salt and pepper, and 2 tablespoons of water, adding some of the spring-onion greens. Whisk the remaining whites to soft peaks and fold into the first egg mixture.

In a wok or non-stick frying pan heat the remaining vegetable oil with the sesame oil. Pour in egg mixture and cook, without stirring, over medium-high heat until the underside is golden-brown and firm. Fold in half, or flip over and cook the other side.

Slide the cooked omelette onto a serving plate and heap with the seafood mixture. Add a swirl of oyster sauce and the remaining spring-onion greens, and serve at once.

SERVES 2

Smoked-salmon bagel
with cream cheese & onion

6 sprigs dill

2–3 tablespoons soft cream cheese

4 fresh bagels

8 slices smoked salmon

1 small red onion, finely chopped

2 teaspoons drained capers

a handful of baby spinach leaves or rocket

Chop 2 of the dill sprigs and stir into the cream cheese. Split bagels, spread both sides with cream cheese and top each base with two slices of smoked salmon. Scatter with the chopped red onion and capers, and top with a few salad leaves. Set upper half of bagel in place, and serve.

MAKES 4

Smoked salmon
& goat's cheese quiche

1 20-cm shortcrust pie base

3 eggs

½ cup sour cream

80 g smoked salmon, cut into strips

70 g soft goat's cheese

1 spring onion, finely chopped

salt and pepper

Preheat oven to 180°C.

Bake the pie crust for 10 minutes, until lightly coloured. Meanwhile, whisk together the eggs and cream, and season with salt and pepper.

Distribute half the spring onion plus the salmon and teaspoonfuls of goat's cheese over the pastry base and pour in the egg mixture. Sprinkle with the remaining spring onion and return to the oven. Cook for about 15 minutes, until the filling is firm to the touch and lightly browned.

Serve warm or cold.

SERVES 3–4

Spaghetti con vongole

350 g dried spaghetti, fettucine or linguini

salt

1 kg clams in their shells

about 1 cup white wine

3 tablespoons olive oil

1½ teaspoons crushed garlic

1 cup tomato and basil pasta sauce

3 tablespoons chopped fresh parsley

black pepper

Boil the pasta in salted water for about 8 minutes, until al dente. Drain.

Steam open the clams (see page 200) in the white wine, then drain (reserve the steaming liquid) and set aside.

Heat the oil in a large pan and sauté the garlic for 40–60 seconds, until fragrant. Add the pasta sauce and the reserved steaming liquid, and simmer for a minute.

Add the parsley and clams, salt and black pepper, and tip into the drained pasta, stirring and tossing until heated and well mixed. Serve in shallow bowls.

SERVES 4

Spaghetti marinara

4 small or 1 large squid tube, cleaned

salt

400 g dried spaghetti (or 500–600 g fresh)

3 tablespoons extra-virgin olive oil

1 small onion, finely chopped

1 × 8-cm stalk celery, diced

3 cloves garlic, finely chopped

½ teaspoon lightly crushed fennel seeds

16 medium-sized raw (green) prawns, peeled and deveined

150 g firm fish fillets, cubed

12 small mussels or clams

2 roma tomatoes, seeded and sliced

½ cup tomato passata (purée)

extra salt and pepper

chopped fresh parsley and basil (or dill)

Cut the small squid tubes into rings (or cut larger squid tube into small squares).

Bring a large pot of water to the boil and salt generously. Add the pasta and boil for about 10 minutes, until al dente. Drain.

Heat the oil in a large non-stick pan and sauté the onion and celery for about 4 minutes, until softened, then add the garlic and the fennel seeds and cook briefly.

Add the prawns and fish to the pan and cook briefly, stirring occasionally and carefully with a wooden spoon. Add the squid and cook briefly, then add the mussels or clams and the tomato slices and passata.

Season to taste with salt and pepper, cover, and simmer for 2–3 minutes until the shells open and flavours are well amalgamated.

Finally, add the drained pasta to the pan and toss over high heat until everything is well mixed.

Serve in bowls, garnished with the herbs.

SERVES 4

Spanish-style casserole of fish with chorizo & capsicum

800 g firm white fish
(e.g. ling or blue eye),
cut into 5-cm chunks

2½ tablespoons olive oil

2 medium-sized onions,
chopped

4 cloves garlic, chopped

2 chorizo sausages, thickly sliced

1 green capsicum, cut into 2-cm
squares

1 fresh hot red chilli, deseeded
and sliced

salt and pepper

2½ teaspoons ground sweet
paprika

2 bay leaves

2 tablespoons chopped fresh
parsley

4 roma tomatoes, sliced
(or 1 cup crushed tomatoes)

¾ cup fish stock

¾ cup fresh breadcrumbs,
mixed with 1 tablespoon
chopped fresh oregano
(or 1 teaspoon dried)

small cubes of butter,
or olive oil

Preheat the oven to 180°C.

Brush a heavy casserole with the oil and place half the fish in the bottom.

In a medium-sized saucepan, sauté the onions in the remaining oil until soft
and lightly coloured (5–6 minutes), stirring frequently. Use a slotted spoon
to transfer onions to the casserole, arranging evenly over the fish. In the
saucepan, now sauté the garlic, chorizo, capsicum and chilli for about ➤

1½ minutes, and transfer it to the casserole. Season with salt and pepper, paprika, bay leaves and parsley. Arrange the remaining fish over the top, cover evenly with tomato slices or crushed tomato, season again and pour in the fish stock.

Cover casserole loosely with aluminium foil brushed with olive oil, and cook in preheated oven for about 25 minutes. After this time, remove the foil, cover the top with the herbed breadcrumbs, and then dot with the butter or drizzle with oil.

Bake for a further 10 minutes, until the crumbs are golden.

Serve in the casserole.

To make fresh breadcrumbs, chop a thick slice of day-old bread and then whiz in a food processor or blender.

SERVES 6–8

Stir-fried spicy seafood with capsicum

3 tablespoons olive oil

1 medium-sized onion, cut lengthways into narrow wedges

½ red capsicum, deseeded and cut into thin strips

½ green capsicum, deseeded and cut into thin strips

a 1-cm piece fresh ginger, peeled and thinly sliced

1 small fresh hot red chilli, deseeded and cut into strips

12 medium-sized green (raw) prawns, shelled (but tail left on) and deveined

8–12 scallops, roe removed

4 small squid tubes, cleaned and sliced into rings

1 tablespoon fish sauce

2 tablespoons sweet chilli sauce

a handful of basil or baby spinach leaves

Heat 2 tablespoons of the oil in a wok until smoking-hot. Separate the onion into layers, then stir-fry with the capsicum until beginning to soften (about 1½ minutes). Remove with a slotted spoon, and set aside.

Add more oil to the wok if needed, add the ginger and chilli and stir-fry briefly. Add the prawns and scallops, and stir-fry over high heat until pink and firm (1½–2 minutes). Add the squid and cook briefly, then add the fish sauce and sweet chilli sauce, and return the onion and capsicum to the wok. Stir-fry until ingredients are glazed with the sauce. Stir in the basil or spinach just before serving.

SERVES 3–4

Tuna & green-olive mousse

½ cup green olives marinated with lemon and garlic

½ cup stuffed green olives

1 × 500-g can tuna in brine, drained

1 cup sour cream

white pepper

1 tablespoon powdered gelatine

Rinse and drain the marinated olives and remove the pits. Place the pitted olives and stuffed olives in a food processor and add the tuna, sour cream and pepper. Process to a reasonably smooth paste.

Stir the gelatine into ½ cup boiling water until dissolved. Add to the tuna mixture in the food processor and mix briefly.

Rinse small moulds or dishes in cold water and spoon in the tuna mixture. Cover, and refrigerate until firm. To serve, turn out mousses and present with a salad of herbs and baby lettuce leaves alongside.

SERVES 8–12

Vietnamese crab & chicken spring rolls

½ cup flaked crab meat

½ cup chicken mince

2 spring onions, very finely chopped

⅔ cup fresh bean sprouts, blanched, drained and chopped

3 teaspoons fish sauce

24 small Vietnamese rice papers (banh trang)

1 tablespoon golden syrup

oil for deep-frying

Vietnamese dipping sauce (page 250)

Combine the crab, mince, spring onions, bean sprouts and fish sauce, mixing well.

Dip rice papers one by one into hot water to soften, and place on a dry cloth. Combine golden syrup with 2½ tablespoons boiling water, and brush lightly over one side of each paper (this glaze makes them turn crisp and golden when fried). Turn rice papers over and place a portion of the crab filling in the centre of each one. Fold up bottom and sides, then roll up firmly.

In a wok or deep pan, heat oil to 190°C and fry the rolls in batches of 6–8, until golden-brown and crisp and the filling is cooked through (about 2½ minutes).

Serve hot with the dipping sauce in small bowls.

MAKES 24

Bugs, crabs, lobsters & prawns

Prawns are an Aussie icon and without doubt the nation's most popular seafood. But don't neglect the other crustaceans — delicious bugs, and sweet-fleshed crabs and crayfish (which include yabbies and rock lobsters).

With whole bugs, crabs and crayfish, most of the edible meat is in the tail. (For this reason, it can be more economical to buy snap-frozen tails, if available, although the flavour will not be the same.) In general, allow 3–4 bugs per person, 4–6 small yabbies (around 60–100 g each), or half a rock lobster. You will only get about 150 g meat from a 500-g crab, but they're worth it. Allow 3–4 prawns per person for entrees and composite dishes, and twice as many when they're the main event.

For basic information on preparing and cooking crustaceans, see page 150.

❮ Barbecued bug tails with garlic herb butter (page 152)

Preparing and cooking bugs, crabs, lobsters and prawns

To split bugs and crayfish in half, insert the point of a sharp, heavy knife or cleaver into the centre of the head and push down towards the tail. Wash gently under running water to rinse away the gut and intestinal tract. To remove tail meat, first twist off and discard the head. With food scissors or a heavy knife, turn the tail upside down and cut along the inside edge on both sides. Pull away the under-shell, then gently lift out the tail meat in one piece.

Blue swimmer and sand crabs can be shelled by hand. Turn the crab upside down, remove the flap underneath, then gently prise off the top shell. Pull away the guts and gills under running water. Pick out the meat with the tip of a knife, pulling away the stiff white membranes. Twist the legs off, crack the claws and carefully slip out the meat.

Spanner and mud crabs have stronger shells and require a heavy knife or cleaver. Crack the claws with a heavy object and carefully extract the meat. Crab meat is easier to extract from cooked crabs than from uncooked.

To boil crustaceans, bring a large pot of salted water to the boil. Add shellfish and bring back to the boil, then reduce heat and simmer. Prawns are cooked when the shells are pink, and the prawns rise to the surface. Drain shellfish immediately after cooking, and immediately chill or cool under running cold water. Approximate boiling times are as follows:

- **bugs** (large) — 8-10 minutes
- **rock lobster** — about 12 minutes
- **freshwater crayfish** (e.g. yabbies, marrons) — ½–1 minute, depending on size
- **blue swimmer, sand and spanner crabs** — large 12–14 minutes / small 10–12 minutes
- **mud crab** — about 15 minutes
- **prawns** — 3–5 minutes

Barbecued bug tails
with garlic herb butter

8 large (or 12 small) Moreton Bay or Balmain bugs

5 tablespoons butter

lemon pepper

salt

3 cloves garlic, crushed

2 tablespoons chopped fresh chives

2 tablespoons chopped fresh parsley or basil

With a sharp knife, split the bugs in half lengthways. Prepare the bug tails (see page 150).

Preheat a barbecue hotplate. Meanwhile, melt the butter in a small saucepan, brush lightly over the cut surfaces of the bug tails and season with lemon pepper and salt. Barbecue for 1 minute.

Add the garlic and chopped herbs to the remaining melted butter and again brush over the cut surfaces of the bugs, then grill, alternately basting and cooking, until done (when ready, the meat will be white and firm).

Serve the bugs, cut side upwards, drizzled with any remaining herb butter.

SERVES 4

Bug salad with avocado & orange

6 cooked Moreton Bay or
   Balmain bugs (or 12 marrons
   or yabbies)
freshly squeezed juice of 1 lime
sea salt flakes and black pepper
1 large ripe avocado, flesh sliced
   thickly

1 orange
1 tablespoon fruity extra-virgin
   olive oil
a few drops of Tabasco sauce
1 small bunch watercress or baby
   spinach

Snap off the bug heads and extract tail meat (see page 150). Cut each tail in half, scraping away the vein, then season with salt and pepper and just a squeeze of lime juice.

Sprinkle avocado slices with a little of the lime juice. Peel the orange and with a sharp knife slice out the segments, working over a bowl to catch the juices.

Make a dressing with the reserved orange juice, the olive oil, salt and pepper, Tabasco to taste, and the remaining lime juice.

Rinse and dry the watercress or spinach leaves, then toss with some of the dressing. Place a little mound of leaves on each plate and arrange bugs, avocado and orange segments over it. Drizzle with the remaining dressing.

SERVES 2–3

Caramel-glazed prawns, Thai-style

125g soft brown sugar

3 tablespoons fish sauce

½ cup water

20 medium-sized raw (green) prawns, shelled and deveined

2 gloves garlic, very finely chopped

½ red onion, very finely chopped

4 spring onions, white and pale-green parts cut into 2-cm lengths

1 tablespoon vegetable oil

¾ teaspoon vegetable oil

1–2 teaspoons chilli oil

4–6 soft lettuce leaves, to serve

To make the glaze, place the sugar, fish sauce and water ina small saucepan and bring to the boil. Simmer for about 4 minutes, stirring occasionally, then remove from heat and allow to cool.

Rinse prawns and pat dry.

Heat a wok over very high heat. Add the oil and when it's smoking, add the garlic and onion, and cook for about 20 seconds. Add the prawns and pepper, and stir-fry for a further 20 seconds. Add 2–3 tablespoons of the caramel glaze with the chilli oil and cook, stirring and turning constantly, until the prawns are well glazed (about 2½ minutes). Add the spring onions and cook briefly, then serve over soft lettuce leaves.

SERVES 4

Chilli crab

1 large fresh mud crab (or several blue swimmer crabs)

3 tablespoons oil

3 cloves garlic, sliced

2 fresh hot red chillies, deseeded and sliced

1 × 2-cm piece fresh ginger, finely sliced

4 spring onions (use white parts and only 6 cm of the greens), chopped

1–2 teaspoons hot chilli sauce or sambal ulek

⅓ cup tomato ketchup

2 teaspoons cornflour

1 cup chicken or fish stock

salt and white pepper

Prepare the crab (see page 150), cutting the body into pieces with a leg attached.

Heat the oil in a wok and add the crab pieces, garlic, chillies, ginger, and spring-onion white parts. Stir-fry over high heat, lifting and turning the crab, until the shell reddens and the crab is almost cooked (about 2½ minutes). Add chilli sauce or sambal ulek to the pan with the tomato ketchup, and stir briefly.

Stir cornflour into the stock and pour into the pan. Simmer, stirring, over high heat until the sauce glazes and the crab is cooked (about 3 minutes). Add the green parts of the spring onions, finely chopped, and salt and pepper to taste. ➤

For maximum impact, serve the crab at the table, piled on a large plate.

In some Singapore seafood restaurants, beaten egg is added to the pan with the stock and is cooked to a creamy, sweetly crab-flavoured custard.

SERVES 4–8

Clear soup with lettuce & crab balls

½ quantity crab and prawn ball mixture (page 169)

4 cups fish or light chicken stock

4 medium-sized cos lettuce leaves

1 tablespoon chopped fresh dill tips or basil

Shape the uncooked crab and prawn mixture into 16 balls and set aside.

In a pan large enough to hold the balls in one layer, bring the stock to the boil. Add the seafood balls, simmer for about 4 minutes, then transfer to soup bowls.

Finely shred the lettuce and drop into the soup with the dill or basil. Cook for about 30 seconds, then divide soup and lettuce between the soup bowls and serve at once.

SERVES 4

Crab & corn soup

1–2 cooked sand crabs or blue
  swimmer crabs

6 cups chicken stock

2 spring onions, sliced at an
  angle (keep white and green
  parts separate)

4 slices fresh ginger, finely
  shredded

1 cup fresh or frozen corn
  kernels

2 teaspoons ginger wine,
  dry sherry or rice wine

1 teaspoon sesame oil

salt and white pepper

1 tablespoon cornflour

1–2 eggs, well beaten

Prepare the crab (see page 150) and extract the meat. Set aside.

Bring the stock to the boil with the spring-onion white parts and half the ginger. Simmer for 2 minutes.

In a food processor, pulse the corn kernels to just break them up (do not purée). Stir corn into the soup with half of the spring-onion greens and the remaining ginger, and bring to the boil. Add wine or sherry, the sesame oil and salt and pepper to taste.

Stir the cornflour into 3 tablespoons of cold water and slowly incorporate into the soup, stirring until it boils and thickens. Add the crab meat and heat for about 1 minute, then remove from the stove. Drizzle the beaten eggs into the saucepan in a thin stream so they set in fine threads.

Serve the soup in bowls and garnish with remaining spring-onion greens.

For a simple summer variation on this soup, replace the corn kernels with 8 asparagus stems, thinly sliced at an angle, parboiled in lightly salted water and then drained.

SERVES 6–8

Crayfish in sweet & tangy sauce

1 large uncooked rock lobster
   tail (or use 4 bugs or 8 large
   prawns)

2½ tablespoons vegetable oil

1 medium-sized onion, cut
   lengthways into narrow wedges

½ red capsicum, cut into 2-cm
   squares

1 Lebanese cucumber, halved
   lengthways, deseeded and
   flesh sliced thickly

1 small fresh hot red chilli,
   deseeded and sliced

a 1.5-cm piece fresh ginger,
   peeled and finely sliced

⅓ cup rice vinegar

⅓ cup white sugar

1½ teaspoons tomato paste

¼ cup water

2½ teaspoons cornflour

salt or fish sauce

½–1 teaspoon cracked black
   pepper

sprigs of fresh coriander
   for garnish

Cut lobster tail in half lengthways and then into thick slices. (If using bugs, also cut in half lengthways.)

Heat the oil in a wok and stir-fry the lobster pieces for about 1 minute, until they are firm. Using a slotted spoon, remove to a plate and set aside.

Add onion and capsicum to the wok and stir-fry for about 1 minute. Add cucumber, chilli and ginger, and stir-fry briefly. Stir in the vinegar, sugar, tomato paste and water, and simmer, stirring, until the vegetables are tender (about 1 minute). ➤

Stir cornflour into an extra 2 tablespoons of cold water and pour into the wok. Add salt (or fish sauce) and pepper and stir until the sauce thickens and becomes translucent. Return the lobster to the sauce and simmer gently for about 30 seconds.

Serve garnished with sprigs of coriander.

SERVES 2

Croque madame with crab

4 thick slices day-old bread

2 tablespoons butter

1½ tablespoons plain flour

1¼ cups milk

1½ teaspoons Dijon mustard

160 g fresh or frozen crab meat, flaked

¾ cup finely grated cheddar cheese

salt and pepper

ground cayenne pepper or ground paprika

Lightly toast the bread and then butter lightly. Set aside on an oven tray.

In a small saucepan, melt the butter and stir in the flour. Cook, stirring, over low–medium heat for 1 minute, then whisk in the milk and mustard. Continue whisking over medium heat until the sauce thickens. Stir in crabmeat and cheese and season to taste with salt and pepper.

Preheat grill to hot. Cover the toast evenly with the sauce and sprinkle with cayenne or paprika. Grill until the topping is bubbling, and serve at once.

SERVES 2–4

Crumbed prawn cutlets

24 medium-sized raw (green) prawns,
 shelled but tails left intact

¾ cup plain flour, seasoned with salt and pepper

2 eggs, well beaten

1¼ cups fine dry breadcrumbs or Japanese panko crumbs
 (see note on page 103)

oil for deep-frying

lemon or lime wedges

tartare sauce (page 248) or chilli lime sauce
 (page 234), to serve

With a sharp knife, cut deeply along the back of each prawn, lift out the dark vein, and press prawns out flat. Lightly coat prawns with the seasoned flour, shaking off any excess.

Place eggs and breadcrumbs in separate shallow bowls. Heat oil to 190°C. Meanwhile, dip prawns first into the eggs, then into the crumbs, coating evenly.

Depending on the size of the pan and depth of oil, slide in 8–12 prawns at a time and deep-fry until golden-brown, turning several times. Retrieve from oil, and drain on paper towels.   >

Serve at once, with lemon or lime wedges for squeezing and the sauce in small dishes for dipping.

- For *Cajun crumbed prawns*, add 1 tablespoon hot Cajun spices to the seasoned flour.
- For *coconut prawns*, make a thin batter with flour, salt and water, dip prawns in the batter then roll them in shredded coconut before deep-frying.

SERVES 2–4

Fried crab & prawn balls

2 slices ciabatta or sourdough
   bread, crusts removed

200 g crab meat

200 g prawn meat

2 spring onions, roughly
   chopped

2 teaspoons freshly squeezed
   lemon juice

1 tablespoon fish sauce
   (or 1–2 anchovy fillets)

2–3 tablespoons chopped fresh
   dill, basil or coriander

salt and pepper

plain flour

oil for deep-frying

chilli lime sauce (page 234)
   or aioli (page 242)

Cut bread into cubes, place in a food processor and chop to coarse crumbs. Add crab meat, prawn meat and spring onions, and process to a paste. Season with lemon juice, fish sauce, herbs and a large pinch each of salt and pepper, and process again until well mixed.

With wet hands, form seafood mixture into small balls. Coat lightly and evenly with flour.

Heat oil to about 170°C, and fry the seafood balls until they rise to the surface and are golden-brown (3½–4 minutes). Drain well, and serve hot with chilli lime sauce or aioli.

MAKES ABOUT 30

Garlic prawns in wine cream sauce

4 cups cooked white rice

3–4 tablespoons butter

1 tablespoon olive oil

1 small onion, very finely chopped

24 large or 32 medium-sized
  raw (green) prawns, shelled
  and deveined

5 cloves garlic, chopped

100 ml dry white wine

300 ml pouring cream

salt and pepper

chopped fresh chives or parsley

Press a cupful of rice at a time into a cup or small bowl, then invert and turn out on individual plates. Set aside or keep in a warm oven.

Heat the butter and oil in a large frying pan and sauté the onion for 2–3 minutes over medium heat, until softened and lightly coloured. Add the prawns and garlic, increase the heat slightly, and sauté, turning and stirring, until the prawns change colour (1½–2 minutes). Remove to a plate.

Pour the wine into the pan and simmer until it evaporates. Return the prawns and add the cream, with salt and pepper to taste. Bring to a simmer and cook gently, stirring occasionally, until the prawns are firm and no longer translucent (about 2 minutes). Add chives or parsley and serve the prawns with the rice alongside.

SERVES 4

Greek prawn & feta casserole

700 g large raw (green) prawns,
    shelled and deveined, but with
    heads and tails left intact

4 spring onions (chop the white
    parts and about 6 cm of the
    greens)

2 cloves garlic, crushed

2 tablespoons fruity olive oil

1 × 400-g can crushed tomatoes

1 teaspoon sugar

salt and black pepper

200 g feta cheese, cut into
    2-cm cubes

3 tablespoons chopped fresh
    parsley

1 teaspoon chopped fresh
    oregano

Preheat oven to 190°C.

Place prawns in a clay pot or casserole and set aside. In a non-stick pan, sauté the spring onions and garlic in the oil until lightly coloured. Add the tomatoes, sugar, salt and pepper, and simmer over medium heat for 2–3 minutes.

Pour this mixture over the prawns, then scatter the feta evenly over, cover, and cook in preheated oven for about 15 minutes. Stir in herbs, check seasoning and take directly to the table, accompanied by rice or mashed potatoes.

SERVES 4

Honey chilli prawns

8–10 large raw (green) prawns, shelled and deveined, but tails left intact

3 cups oil, for deep-frying

about ¾ cup cornflour

2 egg whites

extra 1½ tablespoons cornflour

a pinch of salt

1 small fresh hot red chilli, deseeded and sliced

1½ tablespoons clear honey

1 tablespoon sweet chilli sauce

Dry prawns with paper towels and dust lightly with ½ cup of the cornflour, shaking off any excess. In a wok or deep pan, heat oil to about 170°C.

Meanwhile, whisk egg whites to soft peaks and fold in 1½ tablespoons cornflour plus a pinch of salt. Gently whisk until well combined and smooth.

Holding each prawn by its tail, drag through the batter to coat thickly. Carefully lower prawns into the oil and cook for about 3 minutes, until golden-brown and crisp.

Pour off all but 1 tablespoon of the oil. Add the chilli, honey and sweet chilli sauce, and warm gently until bubbling. Gently turn the prawns in the sauce before serving, or drizzle it over them once plated. Serve at once.

SERVES 2

Japanese steamed egg custards with prawns & lemon (*takara mushi*)

4 dried shiitake mushrooms, soaked in hot water for 15 minutes

3 cups dashi stock (see note below)

2 teaspoons light soy sauce

⅓ teaspoon salt

1 teaspoon sugar

4 eggs, well beaten

1 spring onion, very finely sliced

8 medium-sized raw (green) prawns (or 16 smaller ones), shelled and deveined, but tails left intact

shredded lemon zest

Drain the mushrooms and slice finely.

In a bowl combine the stock, soy sauce, salt, sugar, eggs and half the spring onion. Stir well, and pour into 8 or 16 small pots or Chinese tea cups. Add a prawn to each, leaving the tail exposed. Cover each pot with aluminium foil, set in a steamer and steam over gently simmering water for 2–3 minutes, until almost set.

Sprinkle custards with a few shreds of spring onion and lemon zest, and steam for a further 4–5 minutes. Serve warm.

Japanese dashi stock is available from Asian food stores and some supermarkets, in powdered, paste and liquid form.

MAKES 8–16

Lobster medallions
with dill & limoncello

80 g unsalted butter

1 cooked lobster tail, cut into
   1.5-cm medallions

8 stems asparagus, trimmed

10 small snow peas

1½ tablespoons limoncello
   liqueur (or Pernod)

2 tablespoons chopped fresh
   dill tips

salt and white pepper

moulded rice (see note below)

Heat a sauté pan and melt half the butter over medium heat. Add the lobster pieces and gently warm through for 3–4 minutes.

Meanwhile, steam asparagus and snow peas over gently simmering water for about 3 minutes.

Pour limoncello or Pernod into the pan with the lobster and increase heat to let it bubble. Stir in the dill, salt and pepper, and push the lobster to the side of the pan. Whisk the remaining butter into the sauce.

Unmould the rice onto a serving plate, and arrange the lobster pieces, asparagus and snow peas alongside. Spoon the sauce over and serve with a flourish.

 To make moulded rice, press hot steamed rice into small, oiled, cone-shaped or triangular containers. To unmould, simply invert onto a plate.

SERVES 2

Prawn & avocado nori roll

4 sheets nori (compressed
seaweed)

6–8 lettuce leaves

12 medium-sized to large cooked
prawns, shelled

1 × 180 g salmon fillet

1 large avocado

½ Lebanese cucumber, cut into
long thin strips

¼ cup Japanese pickled ginger,
drained

3 tablespoons mayonnaise

DIPPING SAUCE

2 tablespoons light soy sauce

3 teaspoons freshly squeezed
lemon juice

1 teaspoon wasabi paste

Hold the nori sheets over a gas flame or a hotplate for about 15 seconds,
to soften.

Finely shred the lettuce and arrange over the nori sheets, leaving one
edge uncovered. Place prawns in a line along the centre, parallel to the
uncovered edge. Cut salmon and avocado into strips 1 cm thick, and
arrange beside the prawns. Add cucumber and ginger, spread evenly with
mayonnaise, and roll up each filled sheet, finishing with the uncovered
edge.

Squeeze rolls gently and set, fold-side down, on a plate. Refrigerate for
about 20 minutes, then cut each roll into 5–6 pieces and arrange on a
platter. ➤

For the dipping sauce, simply combine the soy and lemon juice and serve in small dishes, with a small dollop of wasabi alongside.

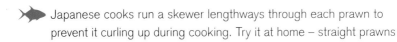 Japanese cooks run a skewer lengthways through each prawn to prevent it curling up during cooking. Try it at home – straight prawns are easier to work with.

MAKES 20–24

Prawn bisque

1.2 kg prawn heads and shells
 (see note on page 183)

2 tablespoons butter or olive oil

1 tablespoon plain flour

1 cup dry white wine

5 cups fish stock

1 tablespoon tomato paste

large pinch of saffron threads
 (optional)

1 teaspoon ground sweet paprika

salt and pepper

12 raw (green) prawns, shelled
 and deveined

½ cup cream

1–2 tablespoons unsalted butter
 (optional)

fresh dill tips for garnish

aioli (page 242 – optional),
 to serve

Place the prawn heads and shells in a heavy saucepan with the butter or oil and brown over high heat for about 5 minutes, shaking the pan frequently. Sprinkle in the flour and use the end of a rolling pin or a cocktail muddler to crush the shells (this extracts the sweet, rich flavour from the heads). Deglaze the pan with the wine, simmering until it evaporates, then add the fish stock, tomato paste, saffron (if using) and paprika, and simmer for about 15 minutes, stirring frequently. Strain the liquid through a fine sieve and discard the shells.

Return stock to the pan, add the prawns and cook for 5 minutes. Season to taste. ➤

Remove several prawns, chop, and set aside for garnish. Purée the remaining prawns and 1½ cups of the liquid in a food processor or blender and return to the saucepan.

Add the cream to the pan and heat gently. Whisk in unsalted butter, if using, and ladle soup into bowls.

Garnish with the chopped prawns and a few dill tips. A dollop of garlicky aioli is a delicious embellishment.

A supply of frozen prawn heads and shells is a great standby for making stock. Simply stash them away in freezer bags each time you shell prawns at home. Defrost before using.

SERVES 6

Prawn & corn fritters

150 g raw (green) prawn meat

½ cup finely chopped onion

½ teaspoon crushed garlic

½ cup fresh breadcrumbs

¾ cup canned corn kernels,
  well drained

¼ cup chopped fresh parsley
  or coriander

2 eggs, beaten

1 cup self-raising flour

½ teaspoon baking powder

1 cup milk

salt and pepper

¼ teaspoon ground hot paprika
  (optional)

¾ cup oil

Chop the prawn meat and combine with all the remaining ingredients
(except the oil) to make a soft batter.

Heat the oil in a pan and fry the fritters in batches over medium heat,
until golden-brown and cooked through (about 1½ minutes on each side).
Drain, and serve hot.

MAKES 24 SMALL OR 12 LARGE

Prawn & haloumi skewers
with basil & tomato dipping sauce

16 medium-sized raw (green) prawns, shelled and deveined

180 g haloumi cheese, cut into 16 cubes

16 long bamboo toothpicks (or short skewers), soaked in hot water for 10 minutes

salt, pepper and ground hot paprika

olive oil

BASIL TOMATO
DIPPING SAUCE

3–4 tablespoons tomato ketchup

1 tablespoon freshly squeezed lemon juice

1½ tablespoons chopped fresh basil

Make the dip by simply combining the ingredients in a bowl. Set aside.

Thread a prawn and a cube of haloumi onto each skewer. Brush with oil and sprinkle with salt, pepper and paprika.

Heat a grill or non-stick pan and grill the skewers over high heat for about 3–3½ minutes, until the prawns are pink and firm and the cheese lightly browned. Arrange on plates over a small salad, or on a serving platter, with the dipping sauce in small dishes.

MAKES 16 (SERVES 4)

Prawn san choy bao

300 g raw (green) prawn meat, finely chopped

3 teaspoons rice wine

1 tablespoon fish sauce or light soy sauce

2 tablespoons vegetable oil

¼ red capsicum, finely diced

3 spring onions, chopped

2 cloves garlic, crushed

1 teaspoon crushed ginger

⅓ cup chopped fresh oyster mushrooms

¼ cup chopped water chestnuts

3 teaspoons sweet chilli sauce

½ cup chicken or fish stock

2 teaspoons cornflour

8 small lettuce leaves

Mix the prawn meat with the rice wine and fish or soy sauce. Set aside.

Heat the oil in a wok and stir-fry the capsicum, spring onions, garlic and ginger for about 2 minutes. Add the oyster mushrooms, water chestnuts and prawn meat and stir-fry for a further 2 minutes, or until the prawn meat is firm and the capsicum tender.

Combine the chilli sauce, stock and cornflour, and stir until thick. Stir through the prawn mixture and place in a dish, with the lettuce leaves served separately so that everyone can fill their own.

MAKES 8 (SERVES 4 AS AN ENTRÉE)

Rice-paper prawn rolls

16 small Vietnamese rice papers (banh trang)

16 medium-sized cooked prawns, shelled

½ punnet snow-pea sprouts (or 1 cup bean sprouts)

1 medium-sized carrot, peeled and cut into matchsticks

1 cucumber, deseeded and cut into matchsticks

16 sprigs fresh coriander or dill

16 large fresh mint leaves

Vietnamese dipping sauce (page 250)

Have ready a bowl of boiling water and a clean dry tea-towel. Dip the rice papers, one at a time, in the boiling water and lift out with tongs when softened (about 30 seconds). Place on the tea-towel. Fold over the top edge of each rice paper.

Place a prawn, a few sprouts, carrot and cucumber sticks and some of the herbs on each wrapper, protruding above the folded edge, and add ½ teaspoon of sauce. Fold up the bottom of the wrapper, then fold the sides inwards to make a firm roll, leaving the top open to expose the filling.

Serve with the remaining sauce, for dipping.

MAKES 16

Sizzling garlic prawns

4 tablespoons unsalted butter

2 tablespoons extra-virgin olive oil

6–8 cloves garlic, finely chopped

24 small to medium-sized raw (green) prawns,
   shelled and deveined but tails left intact

salt and black pepper

chopped fresh parsley for garnish

Preheat the oven to 240°C.

Place a tablespoon of butter in each of four small pots or ramekins.
Divide oil and garlic between the pots and then add the prawns. Season
generously.

Place pots on a tray in the preheated oven and cook for about 7 minutes,
or until sizzling-hot and the prawns pink and cooked through.

Scatter with parsley before serving, and offer plenty of soft fresh bread for
soaking up the delicious garlicky butter.

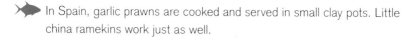 In Spain, garlic prawns are cooked and served in small clay pots. Little
china ramekins work just as well.

SERVES 4

Steamed broccoli
with creamy crab sauce

1 small head broccoli

a 1-cm piece fresh ginger, peeled and shredded

1 small white onion, very finely chopped

1 tablespoon olive oil

90 g crab meat

1½ teaspoons cornflour

¾ cup chicken stock

1 egg white, lightly beaten

salt and white pepper

Break or cut the broccoli into florets and place in a steamer. Cover tightly and steam over simmering water for about 5 minutes until crisp. Tip into a serving dish, cover and set aside.

In a small pan, sauté the ginger and onion in the oil for about 1½ minutes. Add the crab and cook briefly. Stir the cornflour into the chicken stock and pour into the pan, stirring. When the mixture comes to the boil, remove from the heat and drizzle in the egg white in a fine stream so it sets in thin white threads.

Season sauce to taste with salt and pepper, and pour over the broccoli.

SERVES 4

Stir-fried butterfly prawns with ginger & shallots

24 medium-sized raw (green) prawns, shelled and deveined

about 1½ tablespoons cornflour

½ teaspoon bicarbonate of soda

½ teaspoon salt

2 tablespoons oil

a 2-cm piece fresh ginger, peeled and finely shredded

4 spring onions (white parts and 8 cm of greens), cut into 4-cm lengths and shredded finely lengthways

1½ tablespoons light soy sauce or fish sauce

salt and white pepper

½ teaspoon sugar

1 cup water or fish stock

Place prawns in a bowl and add ½ cup water, 2 teaspoons of the cornflour, plus the bicarbonate of soda and the salt. Mix well and leave for 15 minutes (this whitens and crisps the prawns). Drain very well.

Heat the oil in a wok. When smoking, tip in the prawns and stir-fry until they are pink, and beginning to firm up (about 2 minutes). Add the ginger and spring onions, and stir-fry briefly.

Add the soy or fish sauce, salt, pepper and sugar, and cook briefly again.

Stir a tablespoon of the cornflour into the water or stock, pour into the pan and stir until the sauce glazes the prawns. Serve at once.

SERVES 4

Stir-fry of bugs with black beans, garlic & chilli

6 fresh or frozen uncooked
   bug tails

a 3-cm piece fresh ginger

2 teaspoons rice wine or mirin

1½ tablespoons Chinese salted
   black beans

2 cloves garlic, peeled

1 fresh hot red chilli, deseeded

2 tablespoons oil

3 spring onions, chopped

1 tablespoon light soy sauce
   or fish sauce

2 teaspoons cornflour

½ cup fish or chicken stock

If using frozen bug tails, thaw overnight in the refrigerator.

Drain bug tails and pat dry with paper towels. Cut each into three or four medallions and place in a dish. Grate ginger onto a piece of clean cloth and squeeze the juice over the bugs. Sprinkle with the wine or mirin. Turn a few times, then set aside to marinate for about 10 minutes.

Meanwhile, finely chop the black beans, garlic and chilli together.

Heat a wok over high heat and add the oil. Stir-fry the bug tails for about 1½ minutes, until the flesh firms and whitens. Add the chopped black-bean mix and the white and pale-green parts of the spring onions, and stir-fry for 1 minute. Sizzle the soy sauce or fish sauce into the wok and stir-fry a little more.

Stir the cornflour into the stock and pour into the wok. Simmer, stirring, until the sauce thickens and becomes transparent and the bug meat is cooked. Season to taste with salt and pepper, and spread on a serving plate. Garnish with the remaining spring-onion greens and serve at once.

SERVES 4 (MORE IF SHARING SEVERAL DISHES)

Thai salad of crisp-fried prawns

8 large raw (green) prawns, shelled and deveined

a 3-cm piece fresh ginger

salt and white pepper

1 carrot

1 small Lebanese cucumber

1 green apple, cored and grated

1 small red onion, peeled and sliced

2 spring onions, cut into 4-cm lengths and shredded finely

1 large, fresh mild red chilli, deseeded and finely shredded

2 tablespoons fish sauce

3 tablespoons freshly squeezed lemon juice

1 teaspoon sugar

¾ cup self-raising flour

3 cups oil for deep-frying

2 cups mixed small salad leaves

Cut each of the prawns into four, and place in a dish. Grate ginger onto a clean cloth and squeeze the juice over the prawns. Add salt and pepper, and marinate prawns for 10 minutes.

Use a vegetable peeler to shave strips of carrot and cucumber.

Combine, in a bowl, with the apple, onion, spring onions and chilli. Add the fish sauce, lemon juice and sugar, mix well, and set aside. Spread the self-raising flour on a plate.

Heat oil to 190°C in a wok or pan suitable for deep-frying. Remove the prawns from the marinade, drain, and then coat thickly with flour. Deep-fry until crisp and golden (about 2 minutes), retrieve from the oil and drain on crumpled paper towel.

To serve, place a handful of the salad leaves on each plate and top with the marinated salad. Arrange the prawns on top, and dress with the remaining salad dressing.

SERVES 4

Clams, mussels, oysters & scallops

Mussels and clams are among the least expensive seafoods and as a bonus they need minimal preparation and cooking. A few mussels, in their glossy shells, add drama to seafood soups and other composite dishes. Super-fresh oysters really are best eaten straight from the half shell, but they also marry well with tangy flavourings such as soy. Like scallops, oysters should be cooked for the briefest time possible.

Allow about a dozen mussels, clams or pipis per person, more if they are very small. Allow 6–12 oysters per serve as a first course, and 3–4 scallops as an entree and 6–8 for mains.

For basic information on preparing and cooking molluscs, see page 200.

PREPARING AND COOKING CLAMS, MUSSELS, OYSTERS AND SCALLOPS

To open uncooked *clams and mussels*, insert a slim-bladed knife between the shells and cut the muscle holding the creature to its shell.

Clams and pipis are harvested from sand or mud and may contain grit or sand. If not already cleaned by your supplier, soak them overnight in cold water with a few tablespoons of cornflour added. This encourages them to expel any sand trapped within the shell.

Fresh mussels sometimes require cleaning and debearding before cooking. Scrub any crusted shells with a hard brush, or scrape with the back of a knife. Remove the 'beard' (the hairy tuft protruding from the opening of the shell) by gripping firmly with tweezers or between finger and thumb and pulling it away.

Mussels and clams are best cooked by steaming in a tightly closed pot with only a small amount of liquid. Shake the pan often during cooking, as this encourages the shells to open. Open shells means they are cooked: remove immediately from the heat to avoid overcooking, which toughens them. If a mussel feels light and the shell will not open, discard it. Some stubborn shells require longer cooking before they open. Check slow-opening mussels before serving and discard them if they smell strong.

Opening *oysters* is a task best left to the experts, and a good supplier will shuck your fresh oysters to order. Beyond this, oysters need no further preparation before serving or cooking.

Scallops are sold as meat only, with the roe usually still attached, or on the half shell. Scallops off the shell can be cooked in myriad ways; on the shell, they can be cooked in a hot oven, or grilled or barbecued. They require only 3–5 minutes cooking and are ready when the roe is set on the surface and the muscle is white and no longer translucent. Avoid overcooking scallops, as they become dry and even rubbery.

Fresh oysters with Japanese flavours

2 dozen oysters on the half shell

¼ cup dried wakame (Japanese seaweed)

1 tablespoon sliced Japanese pickled ginger
  (reserve 1 tablespoon of the liquid)

1 teaspoon mirin

¼ teaspoon wasabi paste

1 teaspoon light soy sauce

Remove oysters from their shells and set aside. Soak the wakame in warm water until it expands, then drain very well and place a few strands in each oyster shell. Add a scrap of ginger and then return the oysters to the shells.

Mix the ginger liquid with the mirin, wasabi, soy sauce and 2 teaspoons water. Spoon ½ teaspoon of this mixture over each oyster. Serve chilled.

OTHER TOPPINGS FOR OYSTERS ON THE HALF SHELL

· good quality red wine vinegar and freshly cracked black pepper
· lime juice, chopped fresh coriander and a little fresh red chilli
· seafood sauce (page 247)
· salsa verde (page 246)

SERVES 2–4

Grilled spicy mussels

1 kg mussels on the half shell
1 small red onion, very finely chopped
2 cloves garlic, very finely chopped
1 small fresh hot red chilli, deseeded and very finely chopped
3 slices hot pancetta, very finely chopped
2 tablespoons very finely chopped semi-dried tomatoes
salt and freshly ground pepper
¾ teaspoon ground smoked paprika
  (or 1 teaspoon ground sweet paprika)
¾ cup crumbs made from day-old sourdough or ciabatta bread
2–3 tablespoons extra-virgin olive oil

Preheat oven to 220°C, or grill to high.

Loosen the mussels from the shell by sliding a sharp knife under them. Arrange, still in shells, on an oven tray.

In a bowl combine the onion, garlic, chilli, pancetta and semi-dried tomatoes and mix well, seasoning lightly with salt, pepper and paprika. Spread evenly over the mussels, then cover with breadcrumbs and drizzle with oil.   ❯

Place in preheated oven for about 10 minutes, or under grill for about
5 minutes, until the crumb coating is crisp and golden. Serve hot.

Pancetta is a dry-cured Italian ham, available in supermarkets and
delis – you can substitute bacon, but the flavour will be less subtle.
Smoked paprika is favoured in Spanish cuisine for its distinctive,
sweet yet slightly earthy flavour.

SERVES 2–4

Moules mariniere

2 kg mussels in their shells
1 spring onion (white part only), finely chopped
1 tablespoon finely chopped parsley
½ stalk celery (including a few leaves), finely chopped
½ teaspoon fennel seeds (optional)
1 tablespoon butter or olive oil
1½ cups dry white wine
salt and pepper
plenty of chopped fresh coriander or continental parsley

Clean and debeard mussels if necessary (see page 200). Rinse and drain.

In a large saucepan with a tight-fitting lid, lightly sauté the spring onion, parsley, celery and fennel seeds (if using) in the butter or olive oil. Add the mussels and the wine, and cover pan tightly. Bring to the boil and cook, shaking the pan frequently, until the mussels have opened. (This will only take a few minutes: do not overcook, or the mussels will toughen.) With a slotted spoon lift out the mussels and transfer to deep serving bowls.

Season the liquid with salt and pepper to taste, strain over the mussels and scatter with the herbs.

SERVES 4–6

Mussels braised in saffron tomato sauce

3 tablespoons olive oil

1 medium-sized onion, finely chopped

3 cloves garlic, chopped

1 × 400-g can crushed tomatoes

1 green capsicum (or 1½ stalks celery), diced

1 chorizo sausage, diced

a large pinch of saffron threads

1 kg mussels in their shells

salt and pepper

2–3 tablespoons chopped fresh basil, coriander or parsley

Heat the oil in a heavy pan and sauté the onion (and celery, if using instead of capsicum) for about 5 minutes, until well cooked. Add the garlic and sauté briefly, then add the tomatoes, capsicum and chorizo, and simmer for a further 7 minutes or so, adding a little water if mixture is very thick.

Stir the saffron into a litte hot water and leave to steep for about 5 minutes. Add mussels and saffron water to the tomato sauce, with salt and pepper to taste, cover and then cook gently for about 4 minutes or until mussels open. Stir in the herbs just before serving.

SERVES 2–4

Oysters kilpatrick

rock salt

2 dozen oysters on the half shell

2 tablespoons Worcestershire sauce

2 tablespoons butter

$\frac{1}{4}$–$\frac{1}{2}$ teaspoon chilli sauce

3–4 slices rindless bacon, very finely chopped

black pepper

Preheat grill to hot.

Spread rock salt over two ovenproof dishes, and nestle the oysters into the salt.

Gently warm the sauces and butter together, add 1 teaspoon of sauce to each oyster, cover with the chopped bacon and sprinkle with pepper. Place under the grill until bacon is sizzling (about 3 minutes) and serve at once.

SERVES 2–4

Sashimi of scallops with nashi pear & bean-sprout salad

20 large scallops, without roe

¾ cup bean sprouts, peeled and cut into matchsticks

1 spring onion (white part and 4 cm of the greens), very finely chopped

1 small carrot, peeled and cut into matchsticks

zest and juice of 2 limes

3 tablespoons fruity olive oil

1 nashi pear, peeled and cut into matchsticks

1 cup fresh coriander, dill or chervil sprigs

salt and freshly ground black pepper

Chill the scallops in the fridge. Meanwhile, blanch the bean sprouts in boiling water for 20 seconds, drain, refresh in iced water and drain again.

Combine the spring onion, carrot and bean sprouts with the lime juice and olive oil. Leave for 10 minutes, then add the pear, lime zest and coriander, dill or chervil, and season with salt. Leave for a further 10 minutes.

Pat scallops dry with paper towels. With a very sharp knife, cut each scallop horizonally into paper-thin discs and arrange in a ring on plates. Pile a little salad mixture in the centre of each plate, spoon dressing over the scallops, and finish with freshly ground black pepper. Serve lightly chilled.

SERVES 4–6

Scallops grilled on the shell, with lemon beurre blanc

20–24 fresh scallops on the half shell
2 tablespoons butter
salt and freshly ground pepper
lemon beurre blanc (page 239)
chopped fresh chives, dill or parsley

Preheat grill to hot.

Loosen the scallops by sliding a knife between the meat and the shell. Arrange scallops on a baking tray and on each place a small cube of butter and some salt and pepper.

Cook the scallops under preheated grill for about 4 minutes.

Spoon a little of the warm beurre blanc over each scallop, sprinkle with the herbs and serve at once.

SERVES 4

Scallops on the shell
with ginger nectarine salsa

8–12 large scallops on the half shell
sea salt and freshly ground black pepper
olive oil
2 nectarines, peeled and diced
1 spring onion, finely sliced
2–3 teaspoons Japanese pickled ginger, chopped
1 tablespoon chopped fresh mint or coriander
freshly squeezed lime juice

Preheat grill to high.

Arrange scallops on an oven tray, season lightly with salt and pepper, and drizzle with olive oil. Grill for 3–4 minutes, or until firm and no longer translucent. Set aside.

Combine nectarines with the spring onion, pickled ginger and herbs, and season to taste with lime juice, salt and pepper.

When the scallops are at room temperature, cover with the nectarine salsa and serve.

SERVES 4 AS AN ENTRÉE OR 2 AS A MAIN COURSE

Soufflé oysters

2 dozen oysters on the half shell

rock salt

1½ tablespoons butter

4 teaspoons plain flour

½ cup milk

2 eggs, separated

2 tablespoons finely grated parmesan cheese

2 tablespoons finely grated cheddar cheese

2 tablespoons finely chopped chives

crumbs made from 1–2 slices day-old sourdough or ciabatta bread (remove crusts first)

black pepper or ground sweet paprika

Preheat the oven to 220°C.

Spread rock salt over two or four ovenproof plates and place in preheated oven for 6–7 minutes to warm the salt. Remove, and nestle oysters in the salt.

In a small saucepan, melt the butter and then stir in the flour.

Cook, stirring constantly, for about 30 seconds, then whisk in the milk and keep whisking until sauce comes to the boil.

Whisk the egg yolks into the sauce, along with the cheeses and chives. Beat the egg whites to soft peaks and fold these too into the cheese mixture. ➤

Place a spoonful of the mixture on each oyster. Sprinkle a light layer of breadcrumbs over each oyster, and then sprinkle with pepper or paprika.

Place the oysters in the preheated oven for about 5 minutes or until the soufflé mixture puffs and turns a light golden-brown. Serve at once.

SERVES 2–4

Steamed mussels or pipis
with Thai flavours

2 kg mussels or pipis
  in their shells

3 spring onions (white parts
  only), chopped

1 stalk lemongrass, roughly
  chopped

3 kaffir lime leaves,
  torn into pieces

a 3-cm piece fresh ginger,
  cut into chunks

3 cloves garlic, peeled

4 sprigs fresh coriander

1 fresh hot red chilli, deseeded

2 tablespoons fish sauce

1 teaspoon sugar

black pepper

Clean and debeard mussels, if needed (see page 200). If using pipis, purge overnight in salted water to release any sandy residue. Rinse and drain.

Combine all the ingredients in a heavy pan with a tight-fitting lid. Add ½ cup water, cover pan, and cook over high heat until the mussels or pipis open (3–4 minutes), shaking pan frequently. Do not overcook, or the shellfish will toughen.

With a slotted spoon, lift out the shellfish and transfer to individual bowls.

Strain some of the cooking liquid over, then serve.

SERVES 4–6

Cuttlefish, octopus & squid

To be tender, cuttlefish, octopus and squid must be cooked very quickly over high heat or simmered (45 minutes for cuttlefish and squid, and longer for octopus) over low heat. For this reason, grilling/barbecuing and stir-frying, or braising, are ideal cooking methods.

Squid and cuttlefish are both mild in flavour and are inter-changeable in many recipes. If you are buying cleaned tubes, they should be white and unmarked.

For basic information on preparing and cooking cephalopods, see page 220.

❮ Barbecued squid with chilli & herbs (page 222)

PREPARING AND COOKING CUTTLEFISH, OCTOPUS AND SQUID

The smooth dense flesh of cephalopods requires either very brief (no more than 5 minutes) or rather lengthy cooking, to ensure they're tender. Anything in between is almost a guarantee they will be tough.

Fortunately for the squeamish, cuttlefish, octopus and squid can be purchased ready to cook. But cleaning them is easy (if messy) and the gains are freshness and economy.

To clean a squid or cuttlefish, grasp and pull out the head, which will remove the gut. Reach a finger inside and loosen the transparent bone (squid) or white cuttle (cuttlefish), then rinse the whole thing under running cold water. Pull off the skin by gently tugging the flap-like fins. Cut the tentacles and arms away from the head, as these can be eaten. Cut above the eyes, then squeeze out the little hard beak located at the centre of the tentacle base. It is not necessary to skin tentacles.

With baby octopus, cut on either side of the eyes and trim this section away. Squeeze out and cut off the beak. Turn the hood inside out and rinse away the gut and ink sac. Turn right way out again and peel skin from the body pouch and larger arms. Small octopus are left whole; the arms of larger octopus can be sliced. Larger octopus require tenderising before cooking, which is usually done by pounding or by marinating.

Scoring the flesh of squid and cuttlefish improves tenderness and visual appeal. To do so, cut open the body (tube) and place inside surface upwards on a cutting board. With a sharp knife, make a series of diagonal cuts about 8 mm apart, then do the same in the opposite direction to give a cross-hatch effect. This will cause the pieces to curl up into an attractive spiny roll when cooked.

Barbecued squid with chilli & herbs

4 cleaned squid tubes

3 tablespoons olive oil

2 cloves garlic, crushed

1 fresh hot red chilli, deseeded
and sliced

1 fresh mild green chilli,
deseeded and sliced

2 tablespoons chopped fresh
coriander, basil or parsley

4 spring onions, cut into 4-cm
lengths

1 lemon, one half juiced and the
other half cut into wedges

lemon pepper or black pepper

salt

Open out squid tubes and score flesh in cross-hatch pattern (see
page 221). Cut the squid into small pieces.

In a bowl combine the oil, garlic, chillies and herbs. Add the squid and
spring onions, and marinate for 20 minutes.

Meanwhile, preheat a barbecue hotplate or heavy iron pan to smoking.
Tip in the squid, spring onions and marinade, and quickly sear squid on all
surfaces, rolling it across the grill as it begins to curl (about 1–1½ minutes).
Do not overcook, or it will toughen.

Squeeze lemon juice over the squid and serve, with the spring onions, on
a platter. Season with salt and pepper, and accompany with lemon wedges.

SERVES 4

Coconut curry with squid

600g squid tubes

2½ tablespoons vegetable oil

1 onion, finely chopped

2 teaspoons crushed garlic

1½ teaspoons crushed fresh ginger

1½ teaspoons crushed lemongrass

1 teaspoon sambal ulek (chilli paste)

½ teaspoon shrimp paste (blacan)

2 tablespoons ground coriander

2 teaspoons ground cumin

¾ teaspoon ground turmeric

1 × 440-ml can coconut cream

salt

finely shredded kaffir lime leaves, for garnish

Open out squid tubes and score flesh in a cross-hatch pattern (see page 221). Then cut into pieces 4 cm × 3 cm.

Heat the oil in a heavy pan and sauté the onion for about 5 minutes, until softened and coloured. Add garlic, ginger, lemongrass, chilli paste and shrimp paste, and stir for 1–2 minutes until aromatic. Sprinkle in the coriander, cumin and turmeric, and stir for about 30 seconds.

Add the coconut cream, ½ cup water and a large pinch of salt, and bring barely to the boil. Reduce heat and simmer for 6–7 minutes until the onion is quite soft. Add squid and simmer gently for about 5 minutes, until tender. Transfer to a serving dish and sprinkle with shredded lime leaves.

SERVES 4–6

Crunchy cuttlefish strips with five-spice salt

250 g cleaned cuttlefish
  (or squid tubes)

2 teaspoons freshly squeezed
  lemon juice

1 garlic clove, crushed with
  ½ teaspoon salt

2 tablespoons fine table salt

2 teaspoons Chinese five-spice
  powder, or to taste

4 tablespoons cornflour

3 tablespoons rice flour
  or tapioca flour

oil for deep-frying

Rinse and dry the cuttlefish and cut into strips 5 mm × 5 cm. Combine lemon juice, garlic and salt in a bowl with 1 tablespoon of water, add the cuttlefish and marinate for 20 minutes, turning occasionally.

Meanwhile, dry-fry the table salt in a wok for about 1½ minutes. Add the five-spice powder, remove from heat, and shake to mix. Set aside to cool.

Remove cuttlefish from marinade, and dry on paper towels. Combine cornflour and rice or tapioca flour in a plastic bag, add cuttlefish strips and shake to coat. Tip into a colander and shake off excess flour.

Heat oil in a wok or large pan and fry the cuttlefish for about 30 seconds, in small batches, until the coating is crisp and pale golden. Lift out with a slotted spoon and drain on a rack over paper towels. While still hot, toss with the five-spice salt (or serve it separately for dipping).

SERVES 4

Flash-cooked cuttlefish
with cherry tomatoes, rocket & basil

3 cleaned cuttlefish

4 tablespoons olive oil

½ teaspoon crushed garlic

1 teaspoon red wine vinegar

salt and freshly ground pepper

1 punnet cherry tomatoes

1 medium-sized red onion, sliced

2–3 cups baby rocket leaves

8–10 large basil leaves, torn

1 tablespoon freshly squeezed lemon juice

⅓ teaspoon ground paprika

Cut the cuttlefish along one side and fold out flat. With a wide, sharp knife held at a slight angle, cut cuttlefish into very thin slices. Place in a dish and add 1½ tablespoons of the oil, the garlic and the vinegar, and a little salt and pepper. Leave to marinate for 15 minutes.

Cut the cherry tomatoes in half and mix with the onion, rocket and basil. Make a dressing by whisking together the remaining oil with the lemon juice, paprika, salt and pepper.

Heat a barbecue hot plate, wok or heavy iron pan to smoking, and cook the cuttlefish for about 20 seconds on each side. Dress the salad and arrange on plates, drape the cooked cuttlefish over the top, and drizzle with any remaining dressing.

SERVES 3–4

Lemon-pepper squid

3 medium-sized squid, cleaned
½ teaspoon crushed garlic
1½ teaspoons lemon pepper (see note below)
½ teaspoon salt
⅔ cup self-raising flour
3 cups oil for deep-frying

Cut the squid into rings and place in a dish with the garlic, half the lemon pepper and the salt. Mix well and leave for about 10 minutes.

Drain any liquid from the squid and coat rings with flour, shaking off any excess.

Heat the oil and fry the squid for about 40 seconds, until lightly browned. Lift out, drain on paper towels and season with the remaining lemon pepper.

 You can buy lemon pepper in jars in supermarkets, but home-made is better. Simply mash together the finely grated zest of 1 lemon and 2 teaspoons cracked black peppercorns, spread on a baking tray and dry in a low oven (about 100°C). When dried out, grind mixture in a spice grinder.

SERVES 2

Marinated baby octopus with herb & asparagus salad

500 g baby octopus, cleaned

salt

2 tablespoons lemon juice

5 tablespoons olive oil

½ teaspoon crushed garlic

2 sprigs fresh thyme

1 small fresh hot red chilli, deseeded

1 lime, finely sliced

6 asparagus stems

½ cup each coriander, basil and mint leaves

½ cup sliced spring onions

1 cup baby rocket leaves

vinaigrette (page 251)

Blanch the octopus in salted boiling water for 30 seconds, then tip into a colander to drain.

In a saucepan combine the lemon juice, olive oil, garlic, thyme and chilli, ½ cup of water, and the lime slices. Bring to the boil, then remove from the heat and add the octopus.

Leave to cool and marinate for at least 3 hours, or overnight.

Slice asparagus thinly on the diagonal and blanch in boiling, lightly salted water. Drain, chill in cold water, then drain again.

Combine asparagus with the herbs, spring onions and rocket, and dress lightly with the vinaigrette.

Cut larger octopus in half or into four and mix with the salad. Serve on chilled plates.

 For instructions on cleaning baby octopus, see page 221.

SERVES 4

Spicy char-grilled baby octopus

500 g baby octopus, cleaned

1½ teaspoons crushed garlic

1½ teaspoons crushed fresh ginger

½–1 teaspoon crushed red dried chilli

1 teaspoon grated lime zest (or 1 kaffir lime leaf, shredded)

juice of 2 limes

2 tablespoons fish sauce

1 tablespoon oil

2 tablespoons chopped fresh coriander

Rinse and drain octopus, place in a dish and add all the remaining ingredients, stirring to mix well. Cover with plastic wrap and refrigerate for at least 4 hours, or overnight, stirring occasionally.

To cook, heat a barbecue hotplate to very hot. Drain the octopus and cook, stirring frequently, for 2–3 minutes, basting with the remaining marinade. Serve at once.

SERVES 3–4

Extras

While really fresh seafood needs little embellishment, when simply cooked it takes well to subtly spicy, herby and citrusy flavourings.

In this section you'll find versatile sauces from all corners of the globe, as well as classics such as mayonnaise and tartare. There are also recipes for fish and prawn stocks — and, of course, for crunchy potato chips.

< Chilli lime sauce (page 234)

Chilli lime sauce

2 tablespoons freshly squeezed lime juice

2 tablespoons water

1 tablespoon sweet chilli sauce

sugar to taste

Simply combine all the ingredients in a bowl.

MAKES ½ CUP

Crunchy fried potato chips

about 1 kg potatoes (see note below), scrubbed or peeled
about 1 litre canola or vegetable oil for deep-frying

Cut potatoes into chips, parboil in salted water for 3–5 minutes (depending on thickness) and then drain well.

Heat oil to 140°C in a wok or other pan suitable for deep-frying. Slide in the chips in batches and cook, stirring occasionally, until they are pale golden. Lift out with a slotted spoon or wire skimmer and transfer to a wire rack covered with paper towels to drain.

Reheat oil to 190°C, then return chips and fry again until golden. Drain well and sprinkle with salt. Serve at once.

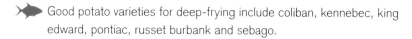 Good potato varieties for deep-frying include coliban, kennebec, king edward, pontiac, russet burbank and sebago.

SERVES 4–6

Fish stock

1 kg fish heads and trimmings

6–8 cups cold water

1 small onion, cut in half

1 small carrot, cut in half

1 stalk celery, cut into chunks

1 bay leaf

sprigs of fresh thyme, rosemary or parsley

Rinse the fish head and trimmings, then drain. Place in a saucepan with all the other ingredients, bring slowly to the boil, and then reduce heat to a gentle simmer. Cook for about 20 minutes (do not allow stock to boil, or it will become cloudy and bitter). From time to time, scoop the scum from the surface with a fine mesh strainer.

Strain, discarding the solids. (The stock can be refrigerated for up to two days, or frozen for up to four months.)

For an Asian-flavoured stock, replace the herbs with sprigs of coriander and a few pieces of lemongrass and fresh ginger. For prawn stock, substitute 500 g prawn heads and shells for the fish, and use 5 cups water. (For a richer version, see the prawn bisque on page 181.)

MAKES ABOUT 1½ LITRES

FISH STOCK

Lemon beurre blanc

¼ cup white wine vinegar

1 tablespoon finely chopped shallots or small pickling onions

1½ tablespoon water

3 teaspoons lemon juice

150 g unsalted butter, cut into small cubes

salt and white pepper

Combine vinegar, shallots and water in a small saucepan and cook until reduced to a few tablespoons. Add the lemon juice and heat briefly, then whisk in the butter a few cubes at a time – keep the sauce barely simmering, and do not allow it to boil. Season to taste, and serve.

MAKES ABOUT ½ CUP

Lime hollandaise

200 g unsalted butter, cut into small pieces
3 egg yolks
2 tablespoons freshly squeezed lime juice
salt and white pepper

First, clarify the butter: place in a saucepan and bring to a simmer, then remove from heat and skim off any scum. Carefully pour into a bowl or jug, leaving any residue behind.

Pour 5 cm of water into a saucepan and bring to a simmer. Combine egg yolks, lime juice and 1 tablespoon of water in a heatproof bowl and whisk well. Place over the simmering water, making sure the bottom of the pan is not touching the hot water. Whisk for 1–2 minutes, using a balloon whisk or electric beater, until eggs are thick and foamy. Slowly add the melted clarified butter, whisking until the sauce is thick and creamy.

MAKES ABOUT 1 CUP

Mayonnaise

1 egg yolk

1½ teaspoons Dijon mustard

a pinch of salt

¾ cup olive oil

1 tablespoon freshly squeezed lemon juice

In a food processor, process the egg yolk with the mustard and salt until creamy. With the motor still running, slowly add about 2 tablespoons of the oil in a very thin stream, and process until it begins to emulsify and turn light and creamy. Slowly add the remaining oil until all is incorporated and the mixture is thick and creamy. Stir in the lemon juice and season to taste with salt and white pepper.

VARIATIONS

- *Aioli (garlic mayonnaise)* – Replace the mustard with 4 cloves of garlic (crushed) and proceed as above.
- *Fennel & mustard mayo* – Substitute ⅓ teaspoon crushed fennel seeds and 2 teaspoons grainy mustard for the Dijon mustard.
- *Wasabi mayo* – Replace the mustard with 2–3 teaspoons of wasabi paste, and add 2 teaspoons light soy sauce.

MAKES ABOUT 1 CUP

Pesto

1 cup firmly packed basil leaves

2 cloves garlic, crushed

2 tablespoons pine nuts

salt

⅔–¾ cup extra-virgin olive oil

2 tablespoons grated parmesan cheese

Combine basil, garlic, pine nuts and a pinch of salt in a food processor and process to a paste. With the motor still running (on low), drizzle in the oil until you have a bright-green, reasonably smooth sauce. Stir in the parmesan.

Pesto will keep, refrigerated, for a day or so in the fridge.

VARIATIONS

- *Rocket pesto* – Substitute baby rocket leaves for the basil.
- *Coriander pesto* – Substitute 1 bunch fresh coriander (leaves only) for the basil, raw cashews for the pine nuts, and 2 teaspoons fish sauce for the parmesan. Season with a little black pepper, and add a squeeze of lemon juice if you like.

MAKES ABOUT 1 CUP

Rouille

4 cloves garlic

salt

1 teaspoon red wine or champagne vinegar

a few drops of Tabasco sauce (optional)

2 egg yolks

about ¾ cup mild-flavoured olive oil

a pinch of saffron threads, steeped
  in 1 tablespoon boiling water

Crush the garlic with a little salt and place in a mortar or small food processor. Add vinegar and Tabasco, and process to a paste. Whisk in the egg yolks and then begin to add the olive oil slowly until mixture is thick, smooth and creamy. Whisk in the saffron and its liquid.

This mayonnaise-like sauce is a traditional accompaniment for seafood soups in Mediterranean France. It will keep for several days in the fridge.

MAKES ABOUT 1 CUP

Salsa verde

1 cup chopped fresh parsley (or use a mix of parsley,
  basil and coriander)

1 clove garlic

2–3 anchovies in oil, drained

1 tablespoon drained capers

1 tablespoon white wine vinegar or
  freshly squeezed lemon juice

3–4 tablespoons extra-virgin olive oil

Place everything in a mortar or small food processor and process
to a chunky paste.

MAKES ABOUT 1 CUP

Seafood sauce

½ cup mayonnaise (page 242)

1 tablespoon tomato ketchup

¼–½ teaspoon Tabasco or chilli sauce

a squeeze of lemon juice

Simply combine all the ingredients in a small bowl, adding the lemon juice to taste.

MAKES ABOUT ½ CUP

Tartare sauce

1 cup mayonnaise (page 242) or sour cream
1 tablepoon finely chopped fresh parsley
1 tablespoon finely chopped capers
1 tablespoon finely chopped fresh chives or tarragon
2 tablespoons finely chopped cornichons (pickled baby gherkins)
a few drops of Tabasco or chilli sauce (optional)
salt and freshly squeezed lemon juice, to taste

Mix everything together, seasoning to taste with salt and lemon juice.

Serve in a bowl or small dishes.

MAKES ABOUT 1¼ CUPS

Vietnamese dipping sauce

$\frac{1}{4}$ cup water

$\frac{1}{3}$ cup fine white sugar

1 small fresh red chilli, deseeded and very finely chopped

1 clove garlic, minced

$\frac{1}{4}$ cup fish sauce

1$\frac{1}{2}$ tablespoons chopped roasted peanuts

2 teaspoons chopped spring onions or fresh coriander

In a small saucepan boil the water and sugar together until syrupy (about 7 minutes). Remove from the heat and add the chilli, garlic and fish sauce. Allow to cool before stirring in the chopped peanuts and spring onion or coriander.

MAKES $\frac{1}{2}$ CUP

Vinaigrette

3 tablespoons extra-virgin olive oil

2 tablespoons white wine vinegar

1 teaspoon Dijon mustard

½ teaspoon crushed garlic (optional)

salt and freshly ground black pepper

Put ingredients in a small bowl and whisk until blended. (Alternatively, place in a small screwtop jar and shake until well combined.) Chopped fresh herbs, particularly tarragon, dill or lemon thyme, are a great addition for salads accompanying seafood.

VARIATIONS

- *Italian dressing* – Omit the mustard, substitute red wine vinegar for the white, and include some chopped fresh oregano or basil.
- *Lemon & soy vinaigrette* – Omit the mustard, substitute lemon juice for the vinegar, and add 1–2 teaspoons light soy sauce.

MAKES ABOUT ¼ CUP

Conversions

Celsius	Fahrenheit
160°C	320°F
170°C	340°F
180°C	360°F
200°C	390°F
220°C	430°F

SIZES

Centimetres	Inches
1 cm	2/5 in
2 cm	4/5 in
2.5 cm	1 in
3 cm	1 1/5 in
4 cm	1 3/5 in
5 cm	2 in
6 cm	2 2/5 in
8 cm	3 in
12 cm	5 in
18 cm	7 in
28 cm	11 in
35 cm	14 in

WEIGHTS

Grams	Ounces
50 g	2 oz
75 g	2½ oz
100 g	3½ oz
120 g	4 oz
150 g	5 oz
200 g	7 oz
225 g	8 oz
250 g	9 oz
300 g	10½ oz
350 g	12 oz
400 g	14 oz
500 g	16 oz (1 lb)
600 g	1 1/3 lb
800 g	1¾ lb
1 kg	2 lb

LIQUIDS

Millilitres	Fluid ounces
100 ml	3 fl oz
200 ml	7 fl oz
400 ml	13½ fl oz
600 ml	20 fl oz (1 pint)

Index

PENGUIN BOOKS

Published by the Penguin Group
Penguin Group (Australia)
250 Camberwell Road, Camberwell, Victoria 3124, Australia
(a division of Pearson Australia Group Pty Ltd)

New York   Toronto   London   Dublin   New Delhi   Auckland   Johannesburg

Penguin Books Ltd, Registered Offices: 80 Strand, London, WC2R 0RL, England

First published by Penguin Group (Australia), 2008

10 9 8 7 6 5 4 3 2 1

Text copyright © Penguin Group Australia 2008

Written by Jacki Passmore

Many thanks to Freedom Furniture in South Yarra, Market Imports and Matchbox (both in Armadale)
for their lovely props.

Cover and text design by Claire Tice © Penguin Group (Australia)
Photography by Julie Renouf
Food styling by Lee Blaylock
Typeset by Sunset Digital, Brisbane, Queensland
Scanning and separations by Splitting Image P/L, Clayton, Victoria
Printed in China by Everbest Printing Co. Ltd

Cataloguing information for this book is available from the National Library of Australia

ISBN 9780 14 300808 8